A LETTER FROM PETER MUNK

Since we started the Munk Debates, my wife, Melanie, and I have been deeply gratified at how quickly they have captured the public's imagination. From the time of our first event in May 2008, we have hosted what I believe are some of the most exciting public policy debates in Canada and internationally. Global in focus, the Munk Debates have tackled a range of issues, such as humanitarian intervention, the effectiveness of foreign aid, the threat of global warming, religion's impact on geopolitics, the rise of China, and the decline of Europe. These compelling topics have served as the intellectual and ethical grist for some of the world's most important thinkers and doers, from Henry Kissinger to Tony Blair, Christopher Hitchens to Paul Krugman, Lord Peter Mandelson to Fareed Zakaria.

Let me say a few words about why we started this program, and why we believe so strongly that the Munk Debates originate out of Toronto, Canada. As a Canadian who wasn't born in this country, a country that has accepted me with open arms and provided me with endless opportunities, I am firmly convinced that Canada must be a vital participant in world affairs. That was the primary reason that Melanie and I helped found the Munk School of Global Affairs at the University of Toronto, my alma mater. It was the same thinking that led my Aurea Foundation to launch the Munk Debates. We wanted to create a forum that attracts the best minds and debaters to address some of the most important international issues of our time, and make these debates available to the widest possible audience. And we wanted Toronto to be at the centre of this international dialogue to affirm Canada's growing role as a world economic, intellectual, and moral leader.

Melanie and I are very pleased that the Munk Debates are making significant strides toward fulfilling the mission and spirit of our philanthropy. The issues raised at the debates have not only fostered public awareness, they have helped all of us become more involved and therefore less intimidated by the concept of globalization. It's so easy to be inward-looking. It's so easy to be xenophobic. It's so easy to be nationalistic. It is hard to go into the unknown. Globalization, to many people, is an abstract concept at best. The purpose of this debate series is to help people feel more familiar with our fast-changing world and more comfortable participating in the global dialogue about the issues and events that will shape our collective future.

I don't need to tell you that that there are many, many burning issues. Whether you talk about global warming or the plight of extreme poverty, or genocide or our shaky global financial order, there are many critical issues that matter to many people. And it seems to me, and to the Aurea Foundation board members, that the quality of the public dialogue on these critical issues diminishes in direct proportion to the importance and the number of these issues clamouring for our attention. By trying to highlight the most important issues at crucial moments in the global conversation, these debates not only profile the ideas and solutions of some of our brightest thinkers and doers, but also crystallize public passion and knowledge, helping to tackle some global challenges confronting humankind.

I learned in life — and I'm sure many of you will share this view — that challenges bring out the best in us. I hope you'll also agree that the participants in these debates challenge not only each other but also each of us to think clearly and logically about important problems facing the world.

Peter Munk
Founder, the Aurea Foundation
Toronto, Ontario

ARE MEN OBSOLETE?

This edition published in 2014 by
House of Anansi Press Inc.
110 Spadina Avenue, Suite 801
Toronto, ON, M5V 2K4
Tel. 416-363-4343
Fax 416-363-1017
www.houseofanansi.com

House of Anansi Press is committed to protecting our natural environment.

Distributed in Canada by
HarperCollins Canada Ltd.
1995 Markham Road
Scarborough, ON, M1B 5M8
Toll free tel. 1-800-387-0117

Distributed in the United States by
Publishers Group West
1700 Fourth Street
Berkeley, CA 94710
Toll free tel. 1-800-788-3123

As part of our efforts, the interior of this book is printed on paper that contains 100%
post-consumer recycled fibres, is acid-free, and is processed chlorine-free.

18 17 16 15 14   1 2 3 4 5

Library and Archives Canada Cataloguing in Publication
Are men obsolete? : the munk debate on gender /
Hanna Rosin, Maureen Dowd, Caitlin Moran, Camille Paglia.
Debate held November 15, 2013, Toronto, Ontario.
Pro: Hanna Rosin, Maureen Dowd;
con: Caitlin Moran, Camille Paglia.

Issued in print and electronic formats.

ISBN: 978-1-77089-451-8 (pbk.). ISBN: 978-1-77089-452-5 (epub)
1. Men — Social conditions. I. Rosin, Hanna, panelist II. Dowd, Maureen,
Panelist III. Moran, Caitlin, 1975–, panelist IV. Paglia, Camille, 1947–, panelist
V. Series: Munk debates
HQ1090.A74 2014   305.31   C2013-906988-7   C2013-906989-5

Library of Congress Control Number: 2013918881

Cover design: Alysia Shewchuk
Text design and typesetting: Colleen Wormald
Transcription: Rondi Adamson

 Canada Council
for the Arts
Conseil des Arts
du Canada

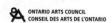 ONTARIO ARTS COUNCIL
CONSEIL DES ARTS DE L'ONTARIO

*We acknowledge for their financial support of our publishing program
the Canada Council for the Arts, the Ontario Arts Council, and the Government of Canada
through the Canada Book Fund.*

Printed and bound in Canada

 FSC
www.fsc.org

MIX
Paper from
responsible sources
FSC® C004071

 ANCIENT FOREST ™
FRIENDLY

ARE MEN OBSOLETE?

ROSIN AND DOWD
VS. MORAN AND PAGLIA

THE MUNK DEBATE ON GENDER

Edited by Rudyard Griffiths

ANANSI

CONTENTS

INTRODUCTION BY RUDYARD GRIFFITHS

The Munk Debate on Gender took place in Toronto on November 15, 2013, in front of a sold-out audience of 3,000 people. The packed concert hall was treated to a remarkable debate, one that ranged from the profound to the uproarious to the profane. Fuelling the hour-and-a-half-long discussion was the debate's contentious resolution, "Be it resolved: men are obsolete." On the surface the motion seems fantastical. Men obsolete, really? If this is indeed the case, what about the 97 percent of Fortune 500 companies with male CEOs? How about the continued dominance of men in politics and a slew of powerful (and high-paying) white-collar professions from medicine to law to finance? And where but in a handful of nations have voters actually elected female heads of state?

These are all important markers of male influence in the early twenty-first century, but the ambit of the Munk Debate on Gender was purposely larger than the power relationship between men and women today. Instead, the debate tackled the surge of female performance relative to men in the home, the workplace, our schools, and society, and addressed the implication of this trend for our collective future.

The rise of women is fast emerging as one of the most important socioeconomic phenomena of our era. In Canada and the United States women make up almost half of the workforce — a threefold increase since the early 1970s. In higher education women now receive 60 percent of the undergraduate and graduate degrees conferred each year, including in previously all-male disciplines such as the sciences, commerce, law, and medicine. At home, modern woman's contribution to child-rearing is off the charts: four out of five single-parent families in the United States are headed by women. More amazing still, women today constitute the single or primary breadwinner in 40 percent of all American families with children under eighteen — a fourfold increase since the 1960s. The dominance of women in child-rearing and family life, their skyrocketing graduation rates at all educational levels, and the reality that they make up an ever-larger portion of the workforce — in both blue- and white-collar professions — all beg the question: What is happening to men?

The decline in performance of men relative to women — a complex and fascinating issue — was the crux of the Munk Debate on Gender. Specifically, are post-industrial nations witnessing a fundamental shift in the status and power of men vis-à-vis women, one that will fundamentally change not just women's place in society but our collective expectations of the role of men in the economy, in family life, and in once traditionally male bastions such as politics? Or are the power structures — economic, cultural, and political — created by men for men, over millennia, still firmly in place, suggesting that men and "maleness" are anything but a spent societal force? To find out, the Munk Debates invited four outstanding women, each of whom has distinguished herself as an original and influential thinker on today's fast-evolving attitudes about gender, to give their analysis of where male/female relations are headed in the twenty-first century.

Arguing for the motion that men are obsolete was the powerhouse duo of Maureen Dowd and Hanna Rosin. Ms. Dowd is the pugnacious and powerful *New York Times* op-ed columnist whose hard-hitting essays and reporting on American politics and culture won her a Pulitzer Prize for journalism. She is also the author of the bestselling book on gender relations, *Are Men Necessary?* This was Ms. Dowd's very first public debate; something one would never have guessed from her uproarious and perfectly timed opening and closing arguments. Maureen's debating partner was no stranger to Oxford Union–style verbal jousting: Hanna Rosin is a national correspondent at *The Atlantic* and a self-confessed high-school debate nerd. She is also the author of the bestselling book on the subject of this debate, *The End of Men.* By weaving original reporting on the lives of average men and women with her own experiences as a mother and spouse, Ms. Rosin has emerged as a leading authority on why women are succeeding in post-industrial societies and men are not.

One pair of stellar debaters deserves another, and in Caitlin Moran and Camille Paglia, the "con" side of the debate had two full-throttle advocates for declaring the demise of men is a fallacious proposition. Ms. Moran is a cultural phenomenon in her own right. She is the author of *How To Be a Woman*, a global bestseller and clarion call for a renewed feminism. Caitlin closely follows contemporary culture as a broadcaster for the BBC and the television critic for *The Times* of London. To the delight of the audience, she brought to the debate her trademark humour and bracing bluntness on issues of sex and gender. Joining Caitlin on the "con" side was iconic writer, commentator, and debating veteran Camille Paglia. The author of a slew of groundbreaking books on gender, history, culture, and sexual identity, Ms. Paglia has distinguished herself as one of the world's top public intellectuals. She is rightly known for her "take no prisoners" debating style and her uncanny ability to marshal an encyclopedic knowledge of history, popular culture, religion, and politics to her arguments.

With the proverbial table set, the debate featured some of the most lively and provocative points, counterpoints, and exchanges in the history of the series.

Hanna Rosin's key argument throughout the debate was that the primary issue at hand is not male versus female power today, since it is obvious that men are currently "on top." Rather, what matters for Hanna is the trend of rising economic success by women and what this foretells for the future of female representation and influence in traditionally male-dominated professions.

For Hanna, the momentum of female success is already evident and will only grow as men struggle to adapt to this new reality: "Women are occupying business positions of power that were once totally closed off to them. . . . Men are the majority of CEOs or popes and so forth; that is absolutely true, but that is just a moment in time, and if you look at the trends, it is completely obvious that world will not last."

Camille Paglia made the first of two rejoinders to this argument. Rather than look at a set of contemporary social trends, Camille reminded readers of the historic role that men played in building Western civilization, from its institutions to its infrastructure to its great works of art. Her core argument was that regardless of the premium post-industrial society puts on knowledge over labour, the role of men as a civilizational force is anything but obsolete: "What is troubling about too many books and articles by feminist journalists in the U.S., despite their putative leftism, is an implicit privileging of bourgeois values and culture . . . It is overwhelmingly men who do the dirty, dangerous work of building roads, pouring concrete, laying bricks, tarring roofs, hanging electric wires, excavating natural gas and sewage lines, cutting and clearing trees, and bulldozing the landscape for housing developments."

Taking up Hanna Rosin's side that men are indeed doomed was the humorous and beguiling Maureen Dowd. The style and content of her interjections were a study in contrast from the other debaters. Instead of evoking a body of facts — historical, cultural, economic, or otherwise — to support her contention that men are obsolete or worse, Maureen used her trademark rhetorical skewering to defuse the initial skepticism of the audience about male decline: "Norman Mailer used to be terrified that women were going to take over the world as punishment for being bad to them over the centuries. All women needed, he said, were about a hundred semen slaves that they could milk every day to keep the race going and have the earth all to themselves. Dream on, Norman! All women need is a few cells in the freezer next to the cherry-flavoured vodka and we're all set."

The job of combatting Maureen Dowd's wooing of the audience through humour and style fell to Caitlin Moran. No slouch herself when it comes to pithy one-liners, Caitlin contended that men would never be obsolete because women would not let them slouch off into the dustbin of history. She believes men and women are moving forward to create gender identities that are not only more fluid, but also more co-operative than in the past. Women can and will have equality with men, and both sexes will benefit from a rebalancing of the power relationship as the stereotypes about what is "male" and what is "female" behaviour fall by the wayside, creating more individual choice for everyone: "Do women gain anything from men becoming obsolete? Do we win by triumphing in work, education, the economy, politics, and business, while retaining our old kingdoms of homemaking and child-rearing? No. Because if that happens, then we will be doing everything! And I don't know about you, but I'm quite knackered. Are men obsolete? My answer is *no*! I won't let you be, you fuckers!"

Part of what makes the Munk Debates as entertaining as they are substantive is the opportunity for audience participation. At the start of the debate the attendees voted on the motion: "Be it resolved, men are obsolete." Eighty-two percent of attendees voted against the resolution. An hour and a half later the audience voted again. The result of the final vote compared to the initial ballot stands out as one of the most surprising in the history of the series. You can now put yourself in the place of the audience. How would you have voted? Would you join the 82 percent in the negative or not? After reading the debate, poll yourself again: Did Camille Paglia and Caitlin Moran confirm your initial assessment of the resolution, or were you in the "pro" camp at the outset? How about Maureen Dowd and Hanna Rosin? Were their arguments convincing or not? This is what makes genuine public debate — free of political and media spin — so important in our information-saturated age. It gives us the time and opportunity to reflect on two sides of an issue cogently and expertly argued and then come to our own conclusion. All of us associated with the Munk Debates hope that you enjoy the humour and rigour of this debate and the contributions of the four remarkable women who took part.

Rudyard Griffiths
Organizer and Moderator, The Munk Debates
Toronto, Ontario

Are Men Obsolete?

Pro: Hanna Rosin and Maureen Dowd
Con: Caitlin Moran and Camille Paglia

November 15, 2013
Toronto, Ontario

THE MUNK DEBATE ON GENDER

RUDYARD GRIFFITHS: Ladies and gentlemen, welcome to the Munk Debates. My name is Rudyard Griffiths and it is my privilege to act as the organizer of this debate series and to once again serve as your moderator. I want to start by welcoming the North America–wide radio and television audience tuning into this debate, everywhere from the Canadian Broadcasting Corporation (CBC) to CPAC, Canada's cable public affairs channel, and throughout the continental United States on C-SPAN. A warm hello also to our online viewing audience tuning into this debate from around the world on munkdebates.com and CBC.ca. It's terrific to have you here as virtual participants in tonight's proceedings. And a warm hello to you, the over 3,000 people who've filled Roy Thomson Hall to capacity for yet another Munk Debate.

All of us associated with this project want to thank you for your enthusiasm for the simple goal to which this series is dedicated: more and better public debate.

Tonight, ladies and gentlemen, we want to expand the focus of our debate for the first time in this series. We want to go beyond geopolitics and international economics to consider one of the big sociological issues of our time — the decline of the performance of men, relative to women, in the family, in the workplace, in schools and universities, and in once all-male bastions such as politics and business. Is this a broad and permanent trend in post-industrial societies such as Canada, one that will fundamentally reshape family life, gender relations, our workplace, and society at large? Or, and it's a big or, are the millennia-old power structures — economic, political, cultural — created by men *for* men still firmly embedded in our society, suggesting that men and maleness are anything but a spent civilizational force? These are the fault lines of tonight's debate, and we've assembled what we think are two pairs of truly outstanding thinkers for your enjoyment and edification.

Their presence on this stage tonight, following some forty-two other debaters since 2008, would not be possible without the generosity and public spiritedness of our hosts tonight. Please join me in showing my appreciation for the Aurea Foundation and its co-founders, Peter and Melanie Munk. This week has been tough for Toronto; the global media can't get enough of Rob Ford, our crack-smoking mayor. At a time like this, civil and substantive conversation takes on added importance, so again, bravo Peter and Melanie Munk, for reminding us what Toronto can and should be all about.

Now, the moment we've all been waiting for. Let's get our debaters out on centre stage and our debate underway. Speaking first, for the motion "Be it resolved: men are obsolete," is Hanna Rosin. She is a national correspondent at *The Atlantic* magazine, and the author of the definitive international bestseller on tonight's topic, *The End of Men*.

Joining Ms. Rosin on the "pro" side of the debate is Pulitzer Prize–winning journalist and author of her own big book on this subject, *Are Men Necessary?* We know her so well as a celebrated *New York Times* columnist. Please welcome Maureen Dowd to the stage and to Toronto — it's her first time in the city.

Now let's get our second team of debaters out here. Rightly lauded as one of the world's top public intellectuals, Camille Paglia is the author of a string of iconic books on gender and culture, and she writes regularly everywhere from the *New York Times* to the *Hollywood Reporter*. Ms. Paglia's debating partner is a phenom in her own right. She is a cultural critic, a TV critic at *The Times* of London, and the author of a global bestseller and new feminist anthem, *How To Be a Woman*. Direct from London, England — Caitlin Moran.

We have a fabulous panel of debaters, but before we get to them and their opening remarks, I want to remind the audience of a house rule: when you see the countdown clock appear on the projection screens at the end of the allotted time for opening and closing statements — six minutes and three minutes, respectively — please join me in a round of applause. This will keep our speakers on their toes, and, more importantly, our debate on schedule.

Finally, let's find out how this 3,000-person audience voted coming into tonight's debate. Our debaters really want to know because they've been asking me about it all day long. In response to the motion "Be it resolved: men are obsolete," 18 percent voted "pro" to 82 percent "con." I'm curious what the response is to our second important question: How many of you would be open to changing your mind depending on what you hear in the next hour and a half? Wow — 77 percent of people say yes; only 23 percent have their minds made up. This is interesting because the Munk Debates are not about one side winning a majority vote — they are about who can swing public opinion, and public opinion is very much in play tonight.

So, it's now time for our debate to formally get underway with opening statements. Our speakers, as I mentioned, have six minutes each, and as is customary the "pro" side will speak first. Hanna Rosin, you're up.

HANNA ROSIN: Wow, there's a surprising number of men out there. That's really not good for us. But we'll do our best.

How do we know men are finished? I'll read you a quote that says it all: "Yeah, there've been times when I've been in a drunken stupor." Your mayor is a shining example of modern manhood, and is what I would call the canary in the coal mine — only he is not quite as delicate as a canary because, as he also shared with us, he's got more than enough to eat at home.

Are men literally obsolete? Of course not. If we had to prove that, we could never win this debate. For one thing, we haven't figured out how to harvest their sperm, without, you know, keeping them alive. But we do have to prove that men, as we have historically come to define them — entitled to power, destined for leadership, arrogant, and confused by anything that isn't them, as in "I don't understand: Is it a guy dressed up like a girl, or a girl dressed up like a guy?" — are obsolete. Okay, that is my last Rob Ford joke. You would do the same if you were me. It's really, really tempting. But I'm going to stop. I'm going to be totally serious now.

It's the end of men because men are failing in the workplace. Over the last few decades, men's incomes have been slowly declining as women's incomes have been slowly rising. Last year, one in five men were not working — something that economists call the greatest social crisis of our generation. This is partly because the global economy has been changing rapidly and men are failing to adjust. But in the meantime women are moving in the opposite direction. In 2009 they became the majority of the American workforce for the first time in history. And now, in every part of America, young single women have a higher median income than single men, which is incredibly important, because it is at the age when men and women are sizing each other up and deciding what their futures are going to look like. As one sorority girl I talked to about her boyfriend put it to me — and remember, sorority girl, not the president of the women's studies centre — "men are the new ball and chain."

It's the end of men because men are failing in schools and women are succeeding. In nearly every country on all but one continent, women are getting about 60 percent of college degrees. Boys start to fall behind as early as first grade and many of them just never catch up. It's the end of men because the traditional household propped up by the male breadwinner is quickly vanishing. Women and men have traditionally learned their social roles at home — man hunter, woman gatherer; man breadwinner, woman homemaker. But the established hierarchy has completely broken down. Now we have a new global type called the alpha-wife: the woman who earns more money than her husband. In the '70s, she was a totally rare breed. And now she's part of about 40 percent of married couples. Women are occupying business positions of power that were once totally closed off to them. The premiers of Canada's four biggest provinces, the head of Harvard, the COO of Facebook, are all women. The newly appointed chairwoman of the Federal Reserve, Janet Yellen, basically got her job because Larry Summers said that women were not that good at math.

But it's not just among the elites. The end of men is even more prominent in the working class. When I speak to working-class communities, the women in the audience look at me like what I'm saying is totally, completely obvious, like the sky is blue or Miley Cyrus is whack. The working class is where men are losing their jobs and losing their roles and their families; women are doing almost everything, creating virtual matriarchies in the parts of the country that used to be our bastions of macho, traditional values. When I asked these women, "Why don't you live with the father of your children?" they said to me, shrugging, "Because he would be just another mouth to feed." I heard this many, many times when I was reporting on the masculinity crisis.

It is the end of men because men have lost their monopoly on violence and aggression. Women are becoming more sexually confident and — something Camille might appreciate — more aggressive in both good ways and bad: going to war, going to jail, playing sports, and, in the case of *The Real Housewives of New Jersey*, beating up anyone who knocks a drink out of their hand.

It's the end of men because men are now obsessed with their body hair, too. In her super-hilarious book, Caitlin catalogues the travails of being a modern woman, one of them being the unacceptability of body hair. If that's the lingering sign of patriarchal oppression, then I counter it with the chest of Anthony Weiner, whom Camille memorably called "a jabbering cartoon weasel," one of my favourite phrases ever. His chest landscape is meticulously tended — there is not a hair anywhere on that body and, as you can imagine, that really, really hurt. And if you were to ask him, "Why are you so shorn, Mr. Weiner?" do you think he would say, "The matriarchy made me do it?" No, he would not, and neither should we.

We don't want to castrate men. We don't want to turn

them into eunuchs. We don't even want to feminize them that much. We just want to keep whatever we love about manhood and adjust the parts that are holding men back. I dedicated my book to my son because he's one of those boys who does get in trouble at school all the time and who thinks the institutions are rigged against him. I believe my job as his mother is not to change him but to accept him for who he is, and to teach him how to adapt to the world as it exists.

So when I think of the world after the end of men, I try to imagine my son in a playground on a Tuesday afternoon and [*audience begins applause*] you get the point.

RUDYARD GRIFFITHS: Wow, what a fabulous start to the debate, Hanna. Camille Paglia, you're up next.

CAMILLE PAGLIA: Good evening. If men are obsolete, then women will soon be extinct, unless we rush down that ominous brave-new-world path where females will clone themselves by parthenogenesis, as Komodo dragons, hammerhead sharks, and pit vipers famously do. A peevish, grudging rancour against men has been one of the most unpalatable and unjust features of second- and third-wave feminism. Men's faults, failings, and foibles have been seized on and magnified into gruesome bills of indictment. Ideologue professors at our leading universities indoctrinate impressionable undergraduates with perilously fact-free theories alleging that gender is an arbitrary, oppressive fiction with no basis in biology.

Is it any wonder that so many high-achieving young women, despite all the happy talk about their academic success, find themselves in chronic uncertainty or anxiety about their prospects for an emotionally fulfilled private life in the early stages of their career? When an educated culture routinely denigrates masculinity and manhood, then women will be perpetually stuck with boys, who have no incentive to mature or to honour their commitments. And without strong men as models to embrace — or for dissident lesbians to resist — women will never attain a centred and profound sense of themselves as women.

From my long observation, which predates the sexual revolution, this remains a serious problem afflicting Anglo-American society, with its puritan residue. In France, Italy, Spain, Latin America, and Brazil, in contrast, many ambitious professional women seem to have found a formula for asserting power and authority in the workplace while still projecting sexual allure and even glamour. This is the true feminine mystique, which cannot be taught but flows from an instinctive recognition of sexual differences. In today's punitive atmosphere of sentimental propaganda about gender, the sexual imagination has understandably fled into the alternate world of online pornography, where the rude but exhilarating forces of primitive nature rollick unconstrained by religious or feminist moralism.

It was always the proper mission of feminism to attack and reconstruct the ossified social practices that had led to wide-ranging discrimination against women. But surely it was and is possible for a progressive reform movement to achieve that without stereotyping, belittling, or demonizing men. History must be seen clearly and fairly. Obstructive traditions arose not from men's hatred or enslavement of women but from the natural division of labour that had developed over thousands of years during the agrarian period and at once immensely benefited and protected women, permitting them to remain at the hearth to care for helpless infants and children.

Over the past century it was labour-saving appliances invented by men and spread by capitalism that liberated women from daily drudgery. What is troubling about too many books and articles by feminist journalists in the U.S., despite their putative leftism, is an implicit privileging of bourgeois values and culture. The particular focused, clerical, and managerial skills of the upper middle-class elite are presented as the highest desideratum, the ultimate evolutionary point of humanity.

Rosin's triumphalism about women's gains [in *The End of Men*] seems startlingly premature, especially given her description of the sagging fortunes of today's working-class couples, that they and we had "reached the end of 100,000 years of human history and the beginning of a new era and there was no going back." This sweeping appeal to history somehow overlooks history's far darker lessons about the cyclic rise and fall of civilizations, which as they become more complex and interconnected also become more vulnerable to collapse.

The earth is littered with the ruins of empires that believed they were eternal. After the next inevitable apocalypse, men will be desperately needed again. Oh sure, there will be the odd gun-toting Amazonian survivalist gal who can rustle game out of the bush and feed her flock, but most women and children will reach out to men to scrounge for food and water and defend the home turf. Indeed, men are absolutely indispensable right now, invisible as it might seem to most feminists, who seem blind to the infrastructure that makes their own work lives possible. It is overwhelmingly men who do the dirty, dangerous work of building roads, pouring concrete, laying bricks, tarring roofs, hanging electric wires, excavating natural gas and sewage lines, cutting and clearing trees, and bulldozing the landscape for housing developments.

It is men who heft and weld the giant steel beams that frame our office buildings. It is men who do the hair-raising work of inspecting and sealing the finely tempered plate glass windows of skyscrapers thirty storeys tall. Every day along the Delaware River, you can watch the passage of vast oil tankers and towering cargo ships arriving from all over the world. These stately colossi are loaded and steered and offloaded by men. The modern economy, with its vast production and distribution network, is a male epic in which women have found a productive role. But women were not its author. Surely, modern women are strong enough now to give credit where credit is due.

RUDYARD GRIFFITHS: That is the Camille Paglia we know and love. Thank you. Maureen Dowd, you are up for your opening statement, please.

MAUREEN DOWD: I've never debated before and I am so screwed.

Even though I grew up in the shadow of the Washington Monument, the jutting, Freudian symbol of the capital under male dominion for centuries, I always knew that men were doomed. That's because I was raised on a steady diet of *femmes fatales*. I love film noir and the films have one inviolable rule: deadly is the female. Guys who could be framed easier than Whistler's mother tangle with women who are trouble, and the guys always end up looking like they took a hayride with Dracula. Film noir is about lady-killers and women who aren't ladies. And the women who aren't ladies wind up killing the lady-killers. The men act like they're under a dark spell, as though they know their futures are all used up and that *femmes fatales* have the right to pursue happiness in all directions. A classic film noir exchange:

Man: "You're never around when I need you."

Woman: "You never need me when I'm around."

These mesmerizing black widows make love to their prey and then consume them, which is actually a fairly common practice in nature. Since we're coming up on Valentine's Day, I'll mention that there are more than eighty species that feature leech babes that devour their male lovers before, during, and after mating. Praying mantises, green spoon worms, and the tiny female midge — who plunges her proboscis into the male midge's head during procreation, her spittle turning his insides to soup that she enjoys as an après-sex snack. Beats a cigarette.

The male orb-weaving spider kills himself before the female has a chance to kill him, turning himself into a plug to prevent other males from copulating, thus ensuring his genes are more likely to live on. Even more ingenious, gene-wise, are the whiptail lizards of the Rio Grande Valley in Texas, who procreate on a purely female basis. No males required. Oh, what a tangled gender-web we weave. As the great Ida Lupino said in *Road House*, "Doesn't it ever enter a man's head that a woman can do without him?"

Women have finally clicked their ruby stilettos three times and realized they have the power. The world is not flat, Tom Friedman. The world is curvy. Norman Mailer used to be terrified that women were going to take over the world as punishment for being bad to them over the centuries. All women needed, he said, were about a hundred semen slaves that they could milk every day to keep the race going and have the earth all to themselves. Dream on, Norman! All women need is a few cells in the freezer next to the cherry-flavoured vodka and we're all set.

Men are so last century. They seem to have stopped evolving, sulking like Achilles in his tent. The mahogany-panelled, McClelland's scotch and rum, *Mad Men* world is disappearing, and the guys are moving into the new androgynous universe more tentatively than women, as they struggle to figure out the altered parameters of manliness and resist becoming house-dudes. Even male genes are refusing to evolve. The once mighty Y chromosome, the demon that yanks us into war and empire-building, has been shedding genes for millions of years and is now a mere remnant of itself and a fraction of the size of its partner, the X chromosome. As Keith Richards told Caitlin, belittling Mick Jagger, whom he calls "Brenda," size matters.

Evolutionary biologists are predicting that in the next 100,000 to 10 million years men could disappear, taking video games, *Game of Thrones* on continuous loop, and cold pizza in the morning with them. The Y chromosome, as renowned evolutionary biologist David Page told me, fell asleep at the wheel 200 million years ago and was headed toward the cliff. But Page and others have now learned that suddenly, about 20 million years ago, the Y chromosome woke up and veered away from the cliff, repairing itself with duplicates of its own genes. Page deduced that the Y said to itself, "I don't have a lot left, but what I have left I'm going to keep." While the Y was shrinking, the X, formerly considered a staid, pristine relic, grew larger and stronger, acquiring new bunches of genes, some of which play roles in producing sperm. So all those centuries, when you guys were asleep at the wheel, we were tinkering under the hood.

When I wrote *Are Men Necessary?* my mom told me to change the title to *Men Are Necessary*, period. "You'll hurt their feelings," she said. So I want to end with a truism the comedian Sarah Silverman tweeted recently: "Dear Men, just because we don't need you anymore doesn't mean we don't want you. Love forever, Women."

RUDYARD GRIFFITHS: One second left, and you said you'd

never debated before. That was absolutely perfect. Well look, it's time to get into our exchange, because —

CAITLIN MORAN: Can I say something?

RUDYARD GRIFFITHS: Oh my God, what have I done? I've totally jumped ahead of you! I was so blown away by Maureen's remarks. But considering you've come all the way from England, I think I should let you speak! My apologies. Caitlin, you're up.

CAITLIN MORAN: I'd like to think that a woman would have remembered to include everyone!

Are men obsolete? If men are obsolete, then I personally aspire to this level of obsolescence — holding 99 percent of the world's wealth; holding sixty-six of the seventy-two spots on *Forbes*'s "Most Powerful People in the World" list; being every single pope, American president, and secretary-general of the UN; and in charge of every military force on earth. If this is men becoming obsolete, I'm intrigued to see what they will be able to achieve once they've downloaded some manner of software update.

I mean, men recorded "Get Lucky" this year, and that is one hell of a catchy record. Men are doing quite well, all things considered. Of course, I understand the general argument here. We basically have a shifting global labour market that increasingly favours someone who can spend ten hours a day wearing a headset, eating Reese's Pieces and making emotionally intelligent chitty chat. We favour them over someone who can break a pig in half with their bare hands.

Whilst men might not currently be obsolescent, the future does look 100 percent female. Except, if true, that would suck as much as when the past was 100 percent male. I don't have many rules in life other than do not eat feta cheese that tastes fizzy, but my big one is be polite. All harm and wrong in the world occurs when people forget to be polite. Ladies, remember how annoyed we were when men said that women were obsolete? How all those millennia of men treating women as second-class citizens seemed impolite? And we took all that Valium and committed self-harm by getting massive perms?

Well, now that we've got a lesbian Icelandic kick-ass president and Sheryl Sandberg in Spanx, let's not do the same thing back to men. Not least because the statistics that suggest that men are becoming obsolete aren't about the kind of men that I *wish* would become obsolete — ass-hats in private jets furthering the various and sundry causes of evil — but essentially working-class men. Given that my feminism is: (a) strident, (b) fuelled by cocktails, and (c) Marxist, I'm kind of not really up for women with soaring prospects dumping on working-class men who are essentially just standing around and going, "Where have all the low-paid jobs in pig-halving gone?" and, "Why is my wife making her hair so huge, dry, and curly? I'm confused and unhappy."

Look, my feminism is neither pro-women nor anti-men but thumbs up for the 7 billion people. Thumbs up for everyone on this little blue-green planet trying to get through the day. In a world of infinite trouble, the idea of equality isn't some fabulous luxury that we can gift ourselves when we are feeling morally flush. Equality is not humanity's cashmere bed socks. It's not a present like champagne. Absolute human equality is a necessity, like water, because if we look at a map of the world where every nation struggling with poverty, child mortality, and political instability is marked in red, it's notable that the bright-red shaming rash coincides almost identically with the most unequal countries in the world.

In the twenty-first century, humanity's greatest resource isn't oil or titanium or gold: it's brains. And any time we make a choice to offline a section of society, we waste these billions of tons of brains. There are a million ways for the world to be better. If women spent the next 100,000 years saying men are obsolete, it would mirror what men said for 100,000 years: women will never happen.

If feminism is the simple, truthful observation that women should be equal to men, then we must do everything to achieve that in the future, whether in some cases it's men helping women achieve equality or in other cases women helping men achieve equality. We urgently need to stop describing things as "problems of men" and "problems of women," and to start seeing all problems for what they are — the "problems of humanity." Women cannot win if men are losing and vice versa, because we all live quite near to each other; we keep having sex with each other and giving birth to each other and being related to each other.

When half of us fall, the other half staggers. If working-class men are struggling, the first people it will impact are working-class women. It's easy to forget this but we are the same species. Women are not from Venus and men are not from Mars. I know because I shared a bunk bed with my brother and, unfortunately for him, I discovered masturbation at that time. He was not 34.8 million miles away.

Anyway, if men do become obsolete, then, as anyone who studies popular culture will tell you, it won't be for long. They'll disappear for ten years until some hipster finds one in a thrift store and goes, "Oh my God, do you remember when we had men? It would be, like, so ironic and amusing if I had one of these back in my house." And suddenly men will be fashionable again and you'll have to pay £900 for them on eBay, and people will start making them out of bits of wire and beads and selling them on Etsy. Do we want that? No.

Think about it. Do women gain anything from men becoming obsolete? Do we win by triumphing in work, education, the economy, politics, and business, while retaining our old kingdoms of homemaking and child-rearing? No. Because if that happens, then we will be doing everything! And I don't know about you, but I'm quite knackered.

Are men obsolete? My answer is *no*! I won't let you be, you fuckers! We are going 50/50 in this world, goddammit, or I'll never have the chance to watch the *Breaking Bad* box set!

RUDYARD GRIFFITHS: Great opening comment, Caitlin, and

I think it's about three in the morning for you, so the profanity absolutely suits the time.

Hanna, I've seen you diligently taking notes throughout these opening statements, and because you spoke first I want to give you the first chance to rebut something that you've heard on the other side. What jumps out at you as saying, "Look, you've got it wrong?"

HANNA ROSIN: Well, just this idea that somehow this is being mean to men. If it were up to me, we would just put all the damn factories back in all the places where the men have lost their jobs. Talking about what is true is not the same as being mean. There is this thing about men where you're never supposed to say that they need any help, or you are never supposed to say that they are suffering in any way because that is mean or degrading them — it's just the truth. We just have to face that a certain kind of men are disappearing from the face of the earth and we've got to try and help them.

CAMILLE PAGLIA: This is very interesting; there is none of the rancour that you spoke of in your book, but there does seem to be an unfairness insofar as the only men who gain voice in your book are those who are willing to confess their victim status. And I felt that there was an absence of the very strong voices of men that I hear as I listen to sports radio, which I do around the clock —

HANNA ROSIN: You listen to sports radio?

CAMILLE PAGLIA: Yes. It is the only place where working-class men can be heard in our culture. Men are calling from trucks, from highways, from construction spots — men who have not graduated from high school but who can analyze in incredible detail exactly what was wrong with the defensive line of the Philadelphia Eagles on Sunday, okay?

HANNA ROSIN: Do you hang out at construction sites?

CAMILLE PAGLIA: Since my first book, *Sexual Personae*, I have sung the praises of construction as a sublime male poetry, and I think that the indifference of upper-middle-class feminists to the actual labour that is going on all around us by these men who are very gallant in their silent service is a distortion —

RUDYARD GRIFFITHS: Okay, Caitlin, let's have you come into this. You are a self-described Marxist, so surely you have a classical Marxist analysis here.

CAITLIN MORAN: Well, first of all, I just want to say that although construction is amazing, I did get ripped off on my double-glazing by the last guys who came and did my windows. You do get recommendations, but not all men are trustworthy builders!

I just want to point out the irony that it has taken four women to discuss the end of men. Why aren't *men* discussing this and working on what they are going to do next? You know, a world where —

HANNA ROSIN: You know why they're not discussing it? Because they're just pretending it's not happening. It drives me nuts.

CAITLIN MORAN: It's just quite funny, though, because we're multi-tasking anyway. We're already doing everything *and* we're also trying to help them out here. It's like, "Come on, you're kind of ending. Get your act together! We want to help you out here!"

RUDYARD GRIFFITHS: But Caitlin, address what is happening in the U.K. as much as in North America. There is a type of man out there who is falling behind in a pretty profound way in education, in work participation, and in family life. What's driving that in society?

CAITLIN MORAN: It must be capitalism, obviously. As I said in my opening statement, I think it is very important that we should stop talking about "problems of men" and "problems of women" and start talking about "problems of humanity." This isn't a question of women overtaking men; it's a question of the economy changing. I think it's a massive diversionary tactic that we phrase it as men against women, whereas it's the underclasses and the peasants that need to revolt against the oppressive —

HANNA ROSIN: I will say I'm fairly neutral on whether the end of men is good or bad. I don't think the end of men is totally awesome and women win and "yay, yay, yay." Some parts of the stuff I describe in my book are terrible, like that there are no dads around, or that women have to do absolutely everything. I'm just saying it's happening; I'm not saying it's awesome. It is just a fact.

RUDYARD GRIFFITHS: But Maureen, let's go to your area of expertise, which is politics. We've got Janet Yellen running the Fed, Christine Lagarde running the International Monetary Fund (IMF), Merkel astride Europe, and Hillary Clinton sizing up the White House in 2016. It looks like we have a bumper crop for women in the world of politics.

MAUREEN DOWD: Bumper crop? Washington has been through a lot in the last thirteen years, and we just seem to be falling ever deeper into the abyss. If Ted Cruz had his way it would be dystopia. The only thing people in Washington are talking about now is not Hillary running against Chris Christie: it's Hillary running against Elizabeth Warren. You know, in politics there's a theory of opposites — that you want the opposite of what you had. Bill Clinton was an emo boy running all over the White House with Monica Lewinsky like the teenagers from *Titanic*, so voters wanted something different; they wanted the macho cowboy in George W. And then he and Dick Cheney smashed the Bush family station wagon into the globe, and that didn't work out. So voters elected a cerebral constitutional lawyer who's supposed to be a tech geek. Once in office he introduces the technological program that's supposed to define his presidency, and it's more *Pong* than *Call of Duty*. So

I think now the opposite approach is to see what the opposite gender can do.

RUDYARD GRIFFITHS: Camille, I want to hear what you think about that. You follow U.S. politics carefully. Have male leaders lost public trust? People seem to be voting with their feet, and they seem to be supporting women.

CAMILLE PAGLIA: Yes, I think people are getting fed up with the endless sex scandals and philandering, and I think there's a sense that somehow woman candidates are not going to be mired down in such things.

But can I just make a point about this dark view of men fading on the world economic landscape? I just don't accept it. Part of my opening statement that I didn't have time to read is that I've been calling for a revalorization of the trades in modern education for twenty years. I feel that there is a very banal, compulsory college track these days, starting in primary schools, funnelling smart students along to a university curriculum that is *extremely* vapid, and what we need is something much more like what is going on in Germany — a co-operation between primary schools and industry, and real vocational training. I think that the upper-middle class has to get over its social snobbery about manual labour, because I've been teaching in an arts —

HANNA ROSIN: I couldn't agree more. I mean, that is why I talk about this stuff. It collides perfectly with the huge problem of income inequality, which is the biggest sin that is going on right now all over the world. You keep saying, these guys are hurting, and you hope that maybe one day somebody will do something about it. I always talk about Germany because Germany has this great respect for the dudes who can make the perfect excellent refrigerator. I wish we had such great respect for those dudes.

CAITLIN MORAN: We keep repeating the same economic cycle over and over again, based on debt and the idea of an infinitely expanding economy, which, logically, cannot be. We also have this belief that progress is always linear, but it often isn't the case. Everything could change in five years if there is more of a decline in manufacturing in Canada and the U.K. I suspect we might realize we need to start making things again rather than just trading invisible debts on the stock exchange. You know, everything that we're talking about tonight could change in the course of two or three years quite easily.

CAMILLE PAGLIA: I have been teaching for forty years at arts schools where people work with their hands. I also come out of Italian-American culture where working with your hands and making beautiful things is valued — not just art objects but things with fabric and metal, leather, and basket-weaving, for instance. And I think that what we need to do is to raise the cultural status of manual labour.

RUDYARD GRIFFITHS: Good point, Camille.

CAMILLE PAGLIA: To me, this is one of the central points of my argument. The low esteem in which working-class men are held is partly due to this shift to a very snobbish, white upper-middle-class elite sensibility.

HANNA ROSIN: But Camille, you always blame this kind of thinking on feminists. Feminists didn't create some fiction about the working-class man. The manufacturing era is over. The working-class man is screwed right now.

CAITLIN MORAN: Can I just stick up for the idea of middle-class elitist, academic feminists — of which I am not one; I never even went to school. Can we not have both? The idea that we could revive both men and women? If men have created something, we can preserve that, and we can keep that going. Then women can go off and create something new and the two can run side by side. It's not like one system has to win over the other.

RUDYARD GRIFFITHS: Like a theme park for men — we can visit and see them working on construction sites.

Maureen, let's have you come in on this point. Manliness today, that iconic image of the construction worker, it's not really as much of the male identity now as it was a generation ago.

MAUREEN DOWD: No, I think we just need to reassure men that they can lie back and relax and relinquish some of the burdens of responsibility that they have carried so sturdily for millennia. Maybe they can try on a frilly apron over their wife-beater T-shirt, to see how fetching it looks while they fetch. Rather than being a boring old necessity, men will now become a luxury, like ice cream.

RUDYARD GRIFFITHS: Now Camille, this is what you rally against — the kind of ornamentalization of men. You believe men are quite different in terms of the trajectory of civilization.

CAMILLE PAGLIA: Yes. In fact, one of the things that rankled me in Hanna's book is the point where she says that men have receded so much that pickup trucks are now mere accessories. It really bothered me because it is simply not true of the contractors who arrive at my suburban house to do the lawn and roof work and whatever else they do. Pickup trucks are not accessories for working-class men.

HANNA ROSIN: Yeah, but I'm talking about Brooklyn — and no doubt Toronto — where you walk into shops that promote a sort of ornamentalized masculinity. The shops sell lumberjack shirts, flasks, and *Playboy*s.

CAITLIN MORAN: Thank you for telling us about these stores because Christmas is coming up and I do need to buy gifts. Where are these places located exactly?

HANNA ROSIN: *Playboy*s from 1962, yours for the asking.

RUDYARD GRIFFITHS: Perfect segue. Let's go to our first video commentator clip. Let's internationalize this debate a bit. We've been talking about North America, but there's an entire world out there. We caught up with Naomi Wolf, third-wave feminist and author of the bestselling book *The Beauty Myth*, among others. Let's have a listen.

NAOMI WOLF: Thank you, Rudyard. Definitely, in some ways, we in the West are in a time when women are making tremendous advances and it is worth noticing. Hanna Rosin's book, *The End of Men*, pointed out that in some professions, like the law, more women are graduating than men — even more than their proportionate number as the majority of the population. Also, as a result of the recent economic downturn in North America that is disproportionately affecting men, working- and lower-middle-class women are increasingly out-earning their husbands or male partners. There have been huge leaps forward in a lot of ways in the West.

But that said, let's take a step back and look at the big picture. We are a fraction of the world's population. If you look at women's status globally, the situation is still appalling. We have so far to go. The routine gang rapes of women in Pakistan and India recently — with no recourse to justice — have been shockingly documented. In places like Thailand and Central Europe, women and girls are trafficked as sex workers with no rights. In places like Saudi Arabia, women can't drive; they don't have full legal rights. And in every corner of the world, women own a fraction of the wealth that men do.

Rather than pit east versus west or men versus women, I'd like to recognize that policies that are good for families, good for girls and boys, good for the environment, good for peace and social justice, are policies that raise the status of women and girls, and educate and invest in them. And when that happens, everybody benefits: communities benefit, the environment benefits, social life benefits. Let's move ahead with supporting the equality of girls and women because it's good for everyone, including men.

RUDYARD GRIFFITHS: Caitlin, let me go to you, because that is very much your message. But if you focus on the international dimension and look abroad to parts of the Middle East and elsewhere, the patriarchy looks alive and well.

CAITLIN MORAN: Yes, my book was banned in the Middle East; apparently, they had parties where they would smuggle it in and read stories about masturbation to each other — hopefully whilst drinking illegal alcohol that they'd smuggled in as well!

This is one of the reasons why I love the Internet. To me, the Internet is female. I think it takes so much time and energy to break into something that has already been constructed, such as patriarchy. The great thing about the Internet is that it opens up this entire new land, this entire continent where women can go to infinitely communicate with each other and join up very quickly.

It takes one teenage activist to start blogging about what's happening, and she can connect with girls all around the world in a way that you never would have before. Previously, if you were the only feminist in your village, you probably wouldn't know any other feminists, but now you can join up and find all the other lonely feminists and start talking about different tactics, ways to activate, and share inspiring stories. And now no girl has to be alone in the world. So this is why I think the Internet is one of the best things to happen to women. On the Internet you are not judged on physicality — no one can see what you look like — you just are simply your thoughts, and the smartest person on the Internet wins; to me that is a brilliant step in evolution as well.

RUDYARD GRIFFITHS: Hanna, you also made an argument in your book that there is a "rise of the woman" phenomenon building in the developing world. Can you share that with us?

HANNA ROSIN: Yes. It's not like every problem has been eradicated everywhere — but the difference now is that unlike even ten years ago, men who commit crimes against women in countries like India are brought to justice. Unlike the Saudi Arabia of ten years ago, there is now an active protest against the law forbidding women to drive. Unlike the world of ten years ago, global bodies like the UN include female quota provisions in policy because they believe women will fix everything. I think we have it in our heads that it is time for women to solve major problems in the developing world, which is very different from how we approached it in the past — patriarchy would have just shut it down straight away.

RUDYARD GRIFFITHS: Camille, do you want to comment on the international dimension of female empowerment?

CAMILLE PAGLIA: As a student of history, I have a sense of foreboding about processes that are at work in the world. With all due respect, I think it is incredibly naive to think that we are moving toward some sort of an economic paradise where women are going to gain control. I think that women's advancement is one of the many things in the West that jihadists consider decadent and would want to target. I've studied the fate of Rome for my entire life. Rome thought it would last forever, but there was a very determined, very fast-moving band of vandals who were able to bring that culture down.

I'm concerned about anything that undermines the identity or prestige of men. I do believe there are going to be political consequences to a culture where women are in charge, because they are generally less militaristic. I think that we are heading toward a nanny state mentality where we cater to social needs now and believe there is no necessity for us to remain vigilant about the future. I'm very concerned.

HANNA ROSIN: So what would you have us do? Just plug the men's ears and pretend it's not happening? Just be like, "It's okay, you're okay?"

CAMILLE PAGLIA: No, I want to build up men's sense of masculine identity again. I want to liberate education. I think that our primary school system is constructed like a prison and that it teaches absolutely nothing except socially approved trendy thoughts.

HANNA ROSIN: Yes, and it totally favours girls, and so until you are actually honest about the boy crisis, until you actually allow people to hear the words "boys are seriously suffering" —

CAMILLE PAGLIA: Right.

HANNA ROSIN: You know, in America people have been talking about the boy crisis since 1990 and we still pretend it's not happening because we can't accept this idea that boys might need help, that boys are suffering.

CAMILLE PAGLIA: Yes.

HANNA ROSIN: It's not okay.

CAMILLE PAGLIA: When Christina Hoff Sommers raised these issues many people said, "Oh, this is not true." Now it's become absolutely conventional wisdom that yes, boys are in crisis. As far as I'm concerned, the way to fix it is to really look at repairing our education system. I think that it is toxic; it is toxic for creativity, it produces clones, it produces people who have been deprived of energy and thought, and we have an extremely mediocre education system that is whittling down male initiative and is compounding this problem. I totally acknowledge Hanna's overall point about this long transition between the old manufacturing base and the white-collar —

RUDYARD GRIFFITHS: But you're agreeing with Hanna. So, do you think this is a moment, a phase that will pass? Do you think qualities of maleness and male identity will reassert themselves, and things will be therefore better in the future?

CAMILLE PAGLIA: No, I'm saying maleness is not going to reassert itself until we revolutionize the education system. I've also been calling for us to look at the way young women are put onto a male track in terms of their own college and graduate and post-graduate education. We allow no wiggle room for ambitious, smart, and talented young women to decide if they would like to have children early. I've been calling for colleges and universities who profess to endorse women's rights to be much more flexible.

RUDYARD GRIFFITHS: That's a very good point, and let's have Maureen weigh in here. Luckily we're not the United States, where you get only a few weeks of maternity leave. There are a lot of structural barriers in American and Western society that prevent women from being as successful as they would like to be, so doesn't that suggest that men aren't obsolete?

MAUREEN DOWD: Yes, obviously we should be more like France in terms of health care for women. But I just want to tell a funny story related to the international situation for women because I've spent a lot of time in Saudi Arabia. I last visited when I was doing a feature for *Vanity Fair* and travelling around. I had read that the grave of Eve, the original Eve, was in Saudi Arabia, so I asked my guide to take me there. He just looked at me like I was crazy and said, "You can't go there; you're a woman." For a second I tried to reason with him and explain why a woman should be allowed to see Eve's grave, but it was no use. Saudi Arabia is still more modern than the Catholic Church; however, there's a lot of work to be done there.

RUDYARD GRIFFITHS: Ouch. Hanna, I can tell you want to come in on this point.

HANNA ROSIN: Which one?

RUDYARD GRIFFITHS: The structural barriers, the short maternity leave, and whatnot. Do you think the very structure of modern professional life is often antithetical to a lot of the things that women want to do and how they want to live?

HANNA ROSIN: We're actually the worst: we don't have any maternity leave that is paid at all, and we're maybe one of three countries that doesn't, which is actually very pathetic. The American workplace doesn't recognize the person as a whole human being who might have other needs. But if I had my druthers, I wouldn't choose the Swedish system, which allows mothers to have a year of maternity leave, because that puts all sorts of pressures on women to behave in a certain way. I believe they actually have a more gender-unequal workplace than we do.

I think we should pursue Sweden 2.0: a kind of gender-neutral proposition that would allow men and women to take time off, which is, I think, what Canada just did. Or do what France does and focus on childcare rather than just maternity leave; create an environment where employers don't just look at women and say, "Oh, they are the ones who are going to screw me and take a year off." It is everybody's job to take care of children, not just women's, even though women do it more.

CAITLIN MORAN: The education system appears to be bad for men and for women. I am someone who was taught at home by my parents, and we just sat around and watched musicals all day and it worked really well for us, so I would encourage everyone to drop out of formal education and just watch *Easter Parade*.

RUDYARD GRIFFITHS: I want to touch on the cultural dimension of this debate. Let's do that by going to the second of our two video contributors. She's an influential political and cultural curator — former editor of *Vanity Fair*, *The New Yorker*, and *Newsweek*. Let's listen to Tina Brown.

TINA BROWN: Thank you, Rudyard. I think Miley Cyrus

and all of her ilk are doing a lousy service to women because they are really just advertising lack of dignity, lack of self-possession, and a kind of gaudy and vulgar way of looking at themselves, which, frankly, just encourages everyone else to look at them that way, too. It seems to me that women have come so far on the one hand, but at the same time are allowing themselves to be dialled back by the wrong kind of pop culture role models.

One of the things that we do at our Women in the World Summit is showcase incredible women who do amazing things for other women; women who are so cool in their own right; women who fight for their education, health, and marriage rights. And then you look at America and see these role models, like Miley Cyrus, who are just so dismal; young women who are just really the wrong people to emulate.

RUDYARD GRIFFITHS: Maureen, I'd like to hear your opinion on this because you write about popular culture a lot. Isn't Miley Cyrus proof positive that a very male, some would say regressive, way of looking at women is still popular? Don't a lot of women feel that they have to conform in order to succeed in the way Miley Cyrus has with her new album?

MAUREEN DOWD: Miley Cyrus is obviously a great marketer, but she doesn't really have a good grasp of what is sexy at all times. As Caitlin said, I would advise her to watch some old movies, maybe '30s and '40s movies, in order to truly understand sex appeal. If she could learn that lesson, she would be a lot more appealing. She should have a little more mystery and hold a little something in reserve.

HANNA ROSIN: But maybe it's like a big "screw you." Maybe she doesn't want to be sexy. She doesn't seem like she wants to be — she is not acting like a girl trying to be really sexy to men.

CAITLIN MORAN: She's not *Pride and Prejudice*, is she? She doesn't seem to be fighting over Mr. Darcy.

HANNA ROSIN: No. No mistake about that.

CAITLIN MORAN: I'm pro Miley Cyrus just gonking about with her whack out because pop music is always going to be about sexiness. It just looks like Madonna to me. She's just out there having a good time. Pop will always be about sex and desire and those kinds of things.

The problem I have with the wider Miley Cyrus thing is the narrowness of the lexicon. Every woman is doing the same act right now. The only two female performers who have been allowed to keep their clothes on in the last five years are Florence Welch, from Florence and the Machine, and Adele. They have been allowed to wear sleeves! It's quite extraordinary. I was trying to explain how weird this all is to a male friend. Every time I turn on MTV both female and male performers have female backup dancers and models twerking and having champagne spread over their asses. I was telling him, "You have to understand how weird it is for me as a woman to see every woman on TV with no clothes on trying to be sexy. It's as if every male pop star you saw on the telly for ten years were obsessed with farming and in every video you saw, they were on a tractor, handling livestock, and were covered in straw."

HANNA ROSIN: But I think there is a male equivalent. They don't have to be farmers; they just have to be thugs. Macklemore and Robin Thicke act like thugs. Like, if there is an ornamental femininity, there is an ornamental masculinity —

CAITLIN MORAN: But they are allowed to be fat; they are allowed to be ugly; they are allowed to wear their clothes in a way a woman can't. Macklemore is not going to be out there with the Botox and capped teeth, is he?

HANNA ROSIN: He's not ugly either, is he?

CAITLIN MORAN: No, but he doesn't have to worry in the same way that women do. I mean, I know the mons of nearly every single female pop star in the world more intimately than I know my own. I have seen them in extreme close-up and detail on MTV. There is a lot of upkeep going on there; these are women who could be fomenting some manner of revolution if they weren't carefully picking out every single piece of stubble with a pair of tweezers before they shoot their new video. It's the simple matter of time devoted to this that I worry about. I think they could be spending more time —

RUDYARD GRIFFITHS: Okay, Camille, come in on this.

CAMILLE PAGLIA: In older movies there were limits set for what could be shown. In fact, those movies formed my own sensibility about sex, which is why I find Miley Cyrus very boring. She is not sexy at all. I mean, I think that she thinks it is sexy. She is going through the motions of sexy. But nothing can compare to the scene in *BUtterfield 8* where Elizabeth Taylor and Laurence Harvey fight in a bar and she grinds her stiletto into the top of his foot, and they have this intense interaction in a public place. Old movies accepted sexual differences, like that great moment in *Gone with the Wind* where all of a sudden Rhett Butler leans on the banister and just looks at Scarlett O'Hara up the stairs. Entire theatres still gasp at that one glance that contains all of male sexuality. It's the best sex scene. So, unfortunately, our problem today is that there is no sizzle left in our films —

RUDYARD GRIFFITHS: But there is no sizzle among guys because —

CAMILLE PAGLIA: I talk about this a lot in my classes at the University of the Arts. Here's the thing — our male actors today don't know how to be men. Why? Because they have watched a whole line of actors ahead of them in film, going back to Brando, and are trying to imitate the men they see on screen. But a lot of these old stars, including Clark Gable, Robert Mitchum, and Charlton Heston, began by working with their hands, and working in factories. So they were real men with real masculine experience that showed up on screen. Gary Cooper is another example.

RUDYARD GRIFFITHS: We're up against time, but I want to give you guys the last word before we go into closing statements. You talked about men and grooming, men looking more like women. Isn't that somehow symbolic of your argument?

HANNA ROSIN: Men have to take care of themselves now. Their hair and beards are a big deal, but you definitely can't have hair in certain places. Hair maintenance used to be an exclusively female problem and now it is everybody's problem. So there is a kind of equal opportunity hair oppression.

RUDYARD GRIFFITHS: Maureen, last word to you.

MAUREEN DOWD: In this political cycle we are spending more time talking about Chris Christie's appearance than Hillary Clinton's, which is a switch.

RUDYARD GRIFFITHS: Following that great discussion, we are going to move into closing statements. As we agreed beforehand, we're going to have closing statements in the opposite order. And this time, I am most certainly not going to forget that Caitlin Moran is going first. You're up — three minutes.

CAITLIN MORAN: Thank you very much. Just a minute ago, I realized that my problem might be that my sexual template is the bit where Bugs Bunny dresses up like a girl and seduces Elmer Fudd — that's essentially what I've based all of my sexual relationships on.

Anyway, two things: (1) life on earth is an experiment; we are a blue-green petri dish. And (2): if you add up all the oppressed minorities of the world — that's all the women, all the LGBT people, all the disabled and all the people of colour — that's about 80 to 90 percent of the world. Straight white men, the patriarchy, have shaped and ruled our world for 100,000 years on what is basically a skeleton staff. They are a tiny proportion of the world. They are basically the night shift, the holiday cover, and in their time they raised the pyramids and put Stonehenge in the middle of the Salisbury Plain, and invented the gods, the car, New York, Twitter, John Frieda Frizz-Ease Serum, and Lycra. Oppression, yes. But you can't deny they got shit done.

So, back to life on earth being an experiment. We have the most fascinating experiment to run right now: (a) see what women turn out to be when they're not afraid and they *are* empowered and they're *not* impoverished and they have achieved equality; and (b) see what is the consequence. What will men turn out to be when they have women as their equals and they can finally debate these things together? How will the triumph of feminism make us all evolve?

I'm so excited to see what little boys will be like when they grow up in a world filled with female presidents and female sports stars and a band that they call the New Beatles, which is all female, and *his* friends scream at *that* band in the way girls used to scream at the Beatles. And how in turn girls will change when they see boys reacting like that. The kaleidoscopic, dizzying wonder of everything that can happen makes me so excited. We are so early in the experiment of what it is to be a human on earth and we have so much to look forward to if we hold our nerve.

We are on the brink of being able to turn into a whole new species. When we merge physically, the old-fashioned way, we make that most astonishing, precious, and awe-inspiring thing: a baby, a new human, a small infinite future. Imagine what we will make when we merge on every level; by merging our intellectual and emotional chemistry into the first-ever society that will be equally male and female, when we collaborate on humanity 2.0 — how this will change our fundamental ideas of gender and sexuality, of what is normal and natural, or what is actually female and male. Basically, I'm imagining a world full of moonwalking pansexual David Bowies and Janelle Monáes, and I've generally never heard of any better plan for the future than that. This is scientifically what we are guaranteed to get if you vote against this motion. Guaranteed. Literally cash back if you don't, although bear in mind I do get on a plane at 6 a.m. tomorrow and my cellphone goes straight to voice-mail. Thank you.

RUDYARD GRIFFITHS: Well done, Caitlin. Up next, Maureen Dowd, with your final three-minute statement.

MAUREEN DOWD: I didn't want to mention this the first time around, given that Canada is my host, but in order to prove definitively that men are not necessary, I only need two words: Ted Cruz. I come here seeking refuge from the apocalyptic terror of Ted Cruz's thunderdome. How on earth did a Canadian almost destroy America? Canadians are usually so nice.

For centuries it was widely thought that women were biologically unsuited to hold leadership positions. It was felt that men best wielded power because men were impersonal, unemotional, forthright, and reasonable. Now it is the highly unstable male temperament that is causing alarm. Male politicians are engaging in sneaky, catty, weepy, ditzy, shrewish behaviour that is anything but reasonable and impersonal. We can't even count on men to be effective tech geeks, given the situation with Obama's rollout on health care.

Women are affected by lunar tides only once a month; men have raging hormones every day, as we noticed when Dick Cheney rampaged around the globe like Godzilla. Rob Ford, your hot mess of a mayor, has had many wild outbursts that, if he were a woman, would certainly be labelled "hysteria," from the Greek for "womb." Who but a hysteric excuses himself for smoking crack by saying he was in a drunken stupor and then talks to reporters about his adventures with lady parts?

I do want one of those bobble-heads, though.

Ted Cruz is a scary mean girl. He threw a hissy fit over Obamacare that shut down the government for sixteen days and cost the American economy $24 billion. Rand Paul, the libertarian senator from Kentucky, grew sulky and needed a fainting couch when Rachel Maddow blasted out that he was a kleptomaniac on Wikipedia. The most emotional member of Congress is Speaker John Boehner, who starts blubbering into his Merlot at the slightest sentimental provocation. Unlike his macho Democratic counterpart, Nancy Pelosi, he's not adept at math and counting; he keeps acting ditzy and bringing Tea Party bills to the floor of the House that do not have the votes to pass.

If you want to talk about catty behaviour, consider this: Ken Cuccinelli refused to call Terry McAuliffe after the Virginia governor's race to congratulate him. Men played so rough and heedlessly with the globe they almost broke it. So we're going in a different direction. Heck, they wouldn't even ask for directions. And no, Sarah Palin, that still does not mean you.

RUDYARD GRIFFITHS: Up next is Camille Paglia. Camille, your three minutes, please.

CAMILLE PAGLIA: I was raised in the 1950s, when it was unheard of for women to be ambitious. The women's movement in the late 1960s paved the way for today's young women — now they feel that every career path is open to them. I am concerned that feminism has painted itself into a corner and is now completely invisible, really. There are sites on the Web that attract committed feminists, but they are completely invisible, and feminism has absolutely no important profile right now in the U.S. I feel that feminism has drifted from any sense of what most people are looking for — value in life.

A career is extremely important, but ultimately, other things become more important as you age. I often walk on the New Jersey shore in a very working-class area, the Wildwoods, and I'm very moved by seeing working-class families, multi-generations, vacationing together. The upper-middle class don't vacation as a family in the same way as the working classes — as people become more affluent they tend to take separate vacations. And I see the joy that elderly people take in what they have wrought. On these multi-generational vacations, the older people there can barely get to the shore or the edge of the water, but are sitting in deck chairs and watching as their grandchildren and great-grandchildren run around.

No matter what you have done in life, no matter what your status, no matter how much power you've achieved — or how much wealth — a point comes where it all feels meaningless. There is nothing left but a sense of what you've contributed to life itself. I am very concerned that the Western obsession with career success, status, and wealth is actually perverting and distorting our sense of the meaning of life itself. I think that feminism needs a major correction back: first of all, by lifting the value of children. There's all this talk about childcare and maternity leave and so on, but in point of fact, the feminist movement, second-wave feminists, in particular, have acted in a way that has tended to denigrate the stay-at-home mom. In fact, its obsession with abortion has made the movement seem as if it is anti-life.

RUDYARD GRIFFITHS: Thank you, Camille. Hanna Rosin, you get the very last word tonight.

HANNA ROSIN: Alright, I'll take it. I think that there is some confusion out there about what you are voting for if you vote for us. When we say men are obsolete that doesn't mean they are worthless, or that we want to stomp on them, or we hate them. It means something different. I'm trying to think about it as being outmoded. Let's say the twin combustion engine technically makes the bicycle obsolete. That doesn't mean that we hate the bicycle or that we want to throw the bicycle away; it just means that you want to use the bicycle exactly how you want to, while recognizing that there is some need for efficiency and change. I think the same is true for men. You are allowed to preserve the parts of manhood that you love and value — whether that is craftsmanship, or macho-ness, or eating nachos and playing video games — whatever it is about manhood that you love you should preserve, while at the same time recognizing that there needs to be some adjustments if men, and particularly certain men, are going to survive in the modern world.

Secondly, I think *you* think that by voting for us you are voting for some kind of crazy, triumphalist feminism; that women have won, and we want to stomp on your car-part jackets and steal your pickup trucks and be really happy about it. But that's not true. It's neither good nor bad; you are just voting as an acknowledgement of a reality. So, when Camille said that we don't recognize these things as valuable anymore, and we don't have vocational programs to respect men, I totally agree with that. But that means that you should vote for our side, because then you are just recognizing the reality of what is going on.

Thirdly, I think that *you* think that if you are voting for us you are somehow blinded to the fact that men are the majority of CEOs or popes and so forth. Yes, they are; that is absolutely true. But if you look at the trends it is completely obvious that this world will not last. I mean, what did Caitlin say about it in her book? "The patriarchy must be knackered by now. It's been 100,000 years without so much as a tea break; let the ladies take over the world for a while." What did Camille say about this? "It is woman's destiny to rule men. Woman is the dominatrix of the universe." Yes! It's true. The energy and the momentum is obviously with women, which doesn't mean that we are crazy, harridan feminists. It just means that we are recognizing the truth.

And, finally, I would say you should just be brave enough to tell the truth about the facts, especially you men out there. Don't pretend it's not happening. I mean, I have a husband who totally still speaks to me, even after a year of me talking about the end of men. I have one son who still speaks to me — and another son who doesn't, but that's beside the fact. I would just say that hiding our heads in the sand and pretending that there is no boy crisis, no crisis in working-class men, and that there isn't a crisis in masculinity, is not the way to go. I would urge you all to acknowledge the truth and vote for us.

RUDYARD GRIFFITHS: Wow! That was a terrific debate. Thank you. The four of you approached this issue with a great combination of wit, insight, and substance. On behalf of the 3,000 people here and all of you watching online, a big thank you.

And again, a big thank you to the Aurea Foundation. The last hour and a half reminded me that yes, Toronto actually is city of sophistication and substance. So bravo, again, Peter and Melanie, for making this possible.

And now for a crucial part of tonight's proceedings: Which one of these teams has been able to sway public opinion in this room? Before you vote for a second time, let's just remind everyone where the numbers stood at the beginning of the evening for the resolution "Be it resolved: men are obsolete." We had 18 percent of voters in favour, 82 percent opposed, and 77 percent were open to changing their vote — a big number. This debate is very much in play.

Those of you at Roy Thomson Hall all have a ballot — and no, you can't use it to kick the mayor off city council, but you can use it tonight for our motion. So please vote wisely and respect the democratic process; vote once.

Summary: The pre-debate vote was 18 percent in favour of the resolution and 82 percent against it. The final vote showed 44 percent in favour of the motion and 56 percent against. Given the shift in votes, the victory goes to the team arguing for the resolution, Hanna Rosin and Maureen Dowd.

Pre-Debate Interviews
with Rudyard Griffiths

CAITLIN MORAN IN CONVERSATION
WITH RUDYARD GRIFFITHS

RUDYARD GRIFFITHS: My name is Rudyard Griffiths and I am the moderator of the Munk Debates. We're doing a series of pre-debate interviews with the fabulous women thinkers who are appearing in tonight's debate: Are men obsolete? Up first is Caitlin Moran, the British author of the bestselling book *How To Be a Woman*, which has stormed the shores here in Canada and in the U.S. Caitlin, it is terrific to have you here.

CAITLIN MORAN: Lovely to be here. You know, you're my first ever Rudyard, so —

RUDYARD GRIFFITHS: Really? I'm surprised. It is, as you know, an English name. There aren't a lot of kids running around —

CAITLIN MORAN: It is one of those things that we exported

and forgot about. We have to come abroad to remember our history.

RUDYARD GRIFFITHS: Hear, hear. Let's start by talking about your very strong support and enthusiasm for feminism, your belief that the struggle for equality should be at the forefront of every woman's thinking.

CAITLIN MORAN: Yes.

RUDYARD GRIFFITHS: Why do you think that a lot of women your age and younger don't share your enthusiasm for that kind of capital-F feminism?

CAITLIN MORAN: Because the word, much like the name "Rudyard," just dropped out of use for a while and everyone just sort of forgot what it meant. I mean, we had feminism up to the early '90s, which was an amazing time for me to be a teenager. Björk, Alanis Morissette, riot grrrl bands, and Courtney Love were our female pop stars, and we used the word "feminism" a lot; even boys used the word "feminism" a lot. Kurt Cobain said, "I'm a big feminist." Then the Spice Girls came along and we stopped using the word "feminist" and we started using the words "Girl Power" instead. And so, for the next generation of girls after me, the word "feminism" is seen as something from history: it is understood as a word about very angry women in dungarees shouting that they hate men. The thing is, I love those shout-y, angry women in dungarees saying, "I hate men." One hundred and fifty years ago, men generally thought that women were on par with animals. We needed a lot of angry women to come along and change things. They gave us the vote and made things like domestic abuse and rape illegal. I'm of the non-angry feminist generation. I find life incredibly amusing. I would like to laugh at the ridiculousness, which is a luxury of modern feminists.

RUDYARD GRIFFITHS: Great answer. What are the new kinds of barriers and boundaries that feminism needs to find to confront and break down? Women have won the right to vote, people are much more conscious of violence against women, at least in the Western world, maybe not so much in India, so where are the new boundaries?

CAITLIN MORAN: I think quotas are a key issue. Although there are many arguments for and against quotas, I'm very much in favour of them in the workplace, including for parliament. People try to argue that if you have quotas that dictate that an organization has to be 50 percent women and 50 percent men, then you will end up with people who are wildly unqualified and who come in and break the photocopier and screw things up. We already have people who are wildly unqualified in the system; people who go to work and break the photocopier, clutter up the office, and screw things up: it's men. If you've got 100 percent men in an office, they're not all going to be amazing — a portion of them are going to be terrible. So why not replace the men who aren't capable with women who are capable? I think it's very important to have 50/50 quotas. It doesn't even matter if some of the women who get in there because of quotas are terrible at their jobs; as anybody who has ever worked in an office knows, you only need three people — max — in there to get anything done. Anyone else who's around is just there in case other people get lonely; you might need someone to chat with on your way to the toilet.

RUDYARD GRIFFITHS: You're opposing tonight's thesis of men's supposed obsolescence. How do you respond to —

CAITLIN MORAN: Aren't you enormously grateful that I'm not saying that men should be exterminated?

RUDYARD GRIFFITHS: Thank you.

CAITLIN MORAN: We're not going to come around and just put you all in big dumpsters —

RUDYARD GRIFFITHS: My Y chromosome will live to see another day.

CAITLIN MORAN: If I win. If I lose, you're doomed! Every single man in this room is [*makes throat-slitting gesture*] at the end of the day.

RUDYARD GRIFFITHS: Yes, give us a bit of a taste of your rebuttal to that kind of argument. Is it that the rise of women isn't a sure thing, or is it that the decline of men is something that is exaggerated, or a bit of both?

CAITLIN MORAN: We can't keep having arguments about men versus women: this is what screws us up. As a feminist, one of the phrases that annoys me the most is "this is a feminist issue." Childcare is a perfect example. If men and women both have to work, as an economic necessity, then the big question is who will look after the children. That is not a "feminist" problem. The issue of childcare obviously affects mankind. We need to stop separating problems into "problems of men" and "problems of women." Every time we describe something as a women's problem, men are like, "Okay, we don't need to bother with that." Or when you say, "This is a problem of men," women go off and do something else. We need to phrase everything in terms of the common humanity — we're in it together. So I think that is the simple answer. I also just have massive residual fondness for men. I live quite near to them; I could give birth to one or even marry one of them; I happen to be related to a few. I've just got some quite good memories of you guys.

RUDYARD GRIFFITHS: But Caitlin, are you concerned that there is a growing underclass of men in the United Kingdom, similar to here in North America —

CAITLIN MORAN: Yes.

RUDYARD GRIFFITHS: Men who are excluded from the workforce, who have lousy scores in terms of educational attainment, in terms of earning power: this is a big sociological issue.

CAITLIN MORAN: Absolutely. I've read Hanna Rosin's book *The End of Men*. It's a very attention-grabbing title. I think a lot of people have sort of mistaken the issue as middle-class women with soaring academic prospects dumping all over working-class men. As someone who comes from a working-class background, my politics are Marxist before anything else, so I'm very against that notion. It is an issue that needs to be identified, so there is no point in ignoring it. Whenever you talk about any sort of societal change, the first few steps involve identifying and describing the problem, and then bringing it to the public discourse, which is what Hanna did with that book. The next thing to do is think about how we want society to be organized. And that is very much what I want to talk about tonight. I think men are struggling in some areas and we need to ask ourselves if we want that; if we don't, then how can we change it? How will change affect us? Will it be good or bad for us?

RUDYARD GRIFFITHS: What is your advice to men? Do you think the workplace has changed to the point that certain female attributes are now better understood and more rewarded materially? Should men discover their feminine side or should men kind of double down on being men?

CAITLIN MORAN: I don't know. I never have any advice for men in the way that I do for women.

RUDYARD GRIFFITHS: But you wrote a whole book for women.

CAITLIN MORAN: Yeah, but —

RUDYARD GRIFFITHS: Help me out here!

CAITLIN MORAN: You're not my normal subject. I really don't know anything about you at all other than what I've seen Luke Skywalker do in *Star Wars*. If you have any problems akin to Luke, like if your aunt and uncle have been killed and your visor has gone out, and you have to rely on the Force to get to the Death Star, I can help you through that, but in terms of working in an iron-hammering factory and balancing that with childcare, I'm all out of ideas. One thing I do know is that it doesn't generally work for women to try and integrate into male realms — women need to find their own space to do things. I think that is why the Internet has been so important, particularly for women trying to break into film and television writing — these genres of writing have been dominated by male narratives. What is really nice about the Internet is that you can be any kind of female you want. Look at all the female activism and other forms of female creativity you see on the Internet. In these cases, women didn't need to break into pre-existing male constructs, we just needed to be given some space and get on with it ourselves. Women are overtaking men in many areas as a result.

For hundreds of thousands of years, men have been doing everything and dominating the discourse, so anything that women say now is generally going to sound quite new, fresh, and weird. Lena Dunham is a perfect example. There are a million more stories like Lena's but we've just never given women the space to vocalize them before.

RUDYARD GRIFFITHS: Two final questions, and do take your time with both: Why has Britain never seen another Margaret Thatcher?

CAITLIN MORAN: Oh, because the first one was so horrible! We all got 'round together in the pub afterwards and said, "Let's not do that one again. That didn't work out too well."

RUDYARD GRIFFITHS: I mean, ideology aside, your country does not do a great job on female leadership.

CAITLIN MORAN: Well, you haven't had any female presidents yet. Have you? I don't know. I haven't checked.

RUDYARD GRIFFITHS: One, briefly, but she wasn't elected. We're working on it. We do have four provincial premiers — the largest provinces, both by economy and population, are now run by women.

CAITLIN MORAN: Alright, you're doing much better than us. The structure of Parliament in Britain is furiously un-female friendly: the long hours, and the fact that everybody has to run down to Westminster to work makes it nearly impossible to balance your life. All the female MPs that I know are campaigning incredibly hard to change that. But yeah, we're rubbish at it and we know it. I mean, no one more than the British likes to sit around and go, "We're British and we're rubbish." So, yes, we are really behind on this.

RUDYARD GRIFFITHS: Finally, is there a man in popular culture, either a fictitious figure or a director, writer, or artist, that you think really gets women right; someone who you think really gets the shifting power dynamic between the sexes?

CAITLIN MORAN: Oh gosh, yes! Well, Joss Whedon, who created *Buffy the Vampire Slayer*. It was amazing. All of his female characters are incredible and he has given several fantastic lectures about writing strong female characters. Russell T. Davies, who rebooted *Dr. Who*, does simple things, like he won't put women in high heels when they are running in a scene, and instead they are just running around in boots. A simple acknowledgement that women can't run in heels makes a big difference!

RUDYARD GRIFFITHS: Especially from a giant space alien.

CAITLIN MORAN: Exactly. Although with zero gravity it might be more likely.

RUDYARD GRIFFITHS: Caitlin, thank you. You've been generous with your time.

MAUREEN DOWD IN CONVERSATION
WITH RUDYARD GRIFFITHS

RUDYARD GRIFFITHS: Welcome, Maureen. It's great to be able to sit down one-on-one with you. Let's jump right into things. Two recent presidents — George W. Bush and Barack Obama — present male identity very differently. What does that say about the larger culture in the United States?

MAUREEN DOWD: It's a really interesting question. The fascinating part about all of it is that they both turned out to be introverts, shockingly enough. George W. Bush started out as this spangly cowboy and Barack Obama was this sleek, modern Spock, and yet they both turned out to be a bit introverted and didn't want to explain things to the American public. George W. didn't want to explain the Iraq War — he just wanted to do it; Obama didn't want to explain his health-care system, or even check out the web site.

RUDYARD GRIFFITHS: Interesting. And do you think these criticisms are fair? Is it accurate to say, "Obama didn't man up?" You have suggested that being president requires a leader to convey a certain charismatic masculinity that you don't see in Obama —

MAUREEN DOWD: I think Democrats are hardest on him, particularly Democrats in Congress. Unlike Ronald Reagan, Barack Obama doesn't understand that you don't just want to be revered, you want to be a little feared, like Lyndon Johnson. How do you use the force of that amazing personality to control Congress? He underestimated that part of the job. A Democratic activist once said that Barack Obama not utilizing his personality is like finding out Bill Gates doesn't like computers. Democrats want Obama to be like Luke Skywalker: they want him to use the Force.

RUDYARD GRIFFITHS: Let's talk about tonight's debate and the collapse of male performance in education, the workplace, and the family. What's going on? Is it outmoded notions of male identity or is there something else that is causing men to underperform?

MAUREEN DOWD: Politically, biologically, and chromosomally, men have basically just stopped evolving. It happened in 1962 or something. Women have been evolving at a really fast clip; even the X chromosome has been speeding ahead of the Y chromosome, which is basically just going off a cliff. I think women have blossomed and men are still struggling with how to blossom. All women want to do is help men into this new era where masculinity is not defined in such rigid terms.

RUDYARD GRIFFITHS: So what do you think men need to do in this new era to succeed? Should men become more feminine or will hyper-masculinity be especially valued? What is the best strategy for that Y chromosome, which is in trouble?

MAUREEN DOWD: I think that you should just do whatever we tell you to do.

RUDYARD GRIFFITHS: Okay, we'll follow advice. You write a lot about popular culture, as well as politics. Is there a man out there, either a fictitious character or a writer-director, that you think really gets women?

MAUREEN DOWD: That's another great question. Funnily enough, I did a great interview recently with James Bond, a.k.a. Daniel Craig. He is in a play with his wife, Rachel Weisz, and we talked a lot about men and women. I asked if billing from the play caused problems between him and Rachel. I assumed James Bond would, of course, want top billing in this play, since he normally makes a lot more money than she does. And he said, no — it has to be equal. So I'm sitting there listening to James Bond talk about equality and I realize that it must be pretty hard for two A-type personalities to be married to each other, both of whom have equally strong careers. He just kept stressing the point that any decision they make has to be good for both of them. That being said, they'll probably be divorced in five years, since it is Hollywood. But at least they live in New York.

RUDYARD GRIFFITHS: So they have hope yet.

MAUREEN DOWD: Yes.

RUDYARD GRIFFITHS: That's a good note to end on. Maureen Dowd, thank you for your time.

MAUREEN DOWD: Thank you. That was so much fun.

HANNA ROSIN IN CONVERSATION
WITH RUDYARD GRIFFITHS

RUDYARD GRIFFITHS: Up next is Hanna Rosin, a national correspondent at *The Atlantic*, author of a big book on tonight's topic, *The End of Men*, and a former high-school debater, is that right?

HANNA ROSIN: That's true. I would like to point out that I am in a room full of men, which always makes the interviews awkward, but that's okay.

RUDYARD GRIFFITHS: So, in a sense, you're the Rembrandt in tonight's debate.

HANNA ROSIN: Because I was a debater in high school? Because I know how to debate? Yes, it was my nerdy life in high school; I spent 80 percent of my time debating around the country, which may not increase my cool factor.

RUDYARD GRIFFITHS: Debating is the new cool. Let's start off by talking about your book, because you have two good analogies for talking about what is going on with gender today. You talk about plastic women and cardboard men. Can you unpack that for us?

HANNA ROSIN: My central thesis is that the global economy is changing really rapidly and for whatever reason a lot of women are having an easier time adjusting to that than men. Is it because women are smarter? Well, no, turns out they're not smarter; men and women test equally. Is it because they are sort of biologically made for this moment? I'm not a biological determinist so I don't actually believe that. After talking to a lot of economists, I came up with this idea that women are just more flexible. It is partly a trait that comes from being the underdog for so long; underdogs are always more adaptable and flexible than the people at the top, who get sort of hardened and rigid. I believe we are at a historical moment in which things have sort of aligned for women. So plastic woman is more flexible; the cardboard man refers to the ways in which men have difficulty being more adjustable and flexible. A lot of this is not just about the economy and the jobs we take; it is also about our conceptions of manhood.

There's a woman who talks about "masculine mystique," and what she means by that is that men are sort of where women were in 1962. In 1962 women were defined in a narrow way — they were put in a little box that made it more difficult for them to move anywhere or do anything. I think there might be a little bit of that going on with men right now because we define masculinity in a narrow way.

RUDYARD GRIFFITHS: That is a key point. In your book, you argue that men are very concerned about their ability to provide for their families, that the role of provider is intimately linked to male concepts of masculinity. In an economy where blue-collar jobs are just shipped overseas, the pillar of masculinity collapses.

HANNA ROSIN: Yes, and that is really important. If you look at our classic feminist texts by Simone de Beauvoir and Germaine Greer, they talk about how women learn that they are like the second sex in the family, that they understand that they are relegated to a certain position because the man knows that he is the breadwinner. So that set-up is really falling apart. More women are providers for their families. The upper classes have sort of remade marriages in a more give-and-take, more equal way. The working classes see that men are just falling off the map — like it's hard for them to find work and they're not really acting as fathers for their children, so that is not as good. But I think that when culture starts to fall apart, a lot of things change. Men and women look at each other completely differently; it is no longer assumed that the man is dominant. The hierarchy falls apart from the way that we have understood it for tens of thousands of years.

RUDYARD GRIFFITHS: Do you think children of all backgrounds, not just the poor, will thrive in this new world of increasingly fatherless families?

HANNA ROSIN: The end–of–men phenomenon feeds into the worst social change that is going on in the world right now, which is the hardening of income inequality. The answer to your question is the same as the answer to almost every question involving income inequality: if you're at the top, the world is your oyster. You get better grades than you ever did, you've got more money than you ever did, your parents pay more attention to you than they ever did. And if you grow up and go to college, life will be much better for you. Beyond the college-educated, which is the vast majority of people — the college-educated make up 30 to 35 percent of the population, depending on the country — your life is much worse. You are far more likely to be living with a single mom, who is probably struggling and doing the best she can. So, your life is a little bit harder, you probably have very little money, and your mom is probably not working a great job. It's not like the end of men means all women are working fabulous jobs. A lot of times they're underpaid, working low-wage jobs, but at least they are working. There's an economist who calls this "the last one holding the bag" theory, which doesn't sound awesome. The mom is left with the kid and she is doing the best that she can. So that is a problem.

RUDYARD GRIFFITHS: What about people from the developing world who are concerned about sexual violence toward women in places like Saudi Arabia, Pakistan, and India. Do you think the rise of women is also unfolding in the developing world?

HANNA ROSIN: Yes, in totally different ways. I get letters that surprise me. For example, I got letters from a group of seamstresses in Gaza who told me that they totally get what I am talking about in my book. They told me that even though we live in totally different worlds, all of the women they know that go to school end up getting their diploma or degree while the men don't stay in school. They said they won't let men tell them who to marry. So, does that mean that women in Gaza are totally liberated and get to do what they want and have sex like they want or are even on the path to being like us? No. But look at Liberia as an example, a war-torn country where they have suddenly decided that women are going to save everything. International aid organizations are big into female quotas in politics because there is this sense in the international aid world that we need women to come in and rescue things. So, it's not the same as it is here but we do have the sense that the energy is with women, and the changes are with women. But no, it's not feminist liberation like in America circa 1975.

RUDYARD GRIFFITHS: You mention in your book that South Korean families would rather have a daughter than a son, which is interesting because up until very recently the country would have been considered quite patriarchal. What is driving that?

HANNA ROSIN: That is my absolute favourite statistic in my whole book because it was so surprising.

RUDYARD GRIFFITHS: That blew me away. I hope you use it tonight.

HANNA ROSIN: Yes, a statistician who had listened to my radio show at *Slate* gave it to me. I had mentioned that I was going to Korea and he emailed me and said that he had all the Koreans' data from the last fifty years.

South Korea remains a thoroughly patriarchal society — you will not find one single woman at the top of any of these huge corporations. On the other hand, the rise of women has caused tremendous social disruption in the country: laws, universities, the age at which people get married — many Korean women don't want to get married and assume the traditional Korean wife role — have all changed. So you have a situation where women are rising but the culture won't; it's just rumbling and rumbling. The culture won't let it happen, like in Japan. The one major thing that has changed is that the preference for the first-born child has totally flipped, which has really been in the last couple of years, so that couples now say they would rather have a daughter than a son.

RUDYARD GRIFFITHS: This is a key part of your argument, which is that it is really about trends. It doesn't just look at how many women are CEOs of Fortune 500 companies; it's about a line stretching out into the future that shows that women are going to do pretty well for the coming century.

HANNA ROSIN: I've never been in a debate where I'm not talking about CEOs, but to me it's the least interesting and least imaginative way to approach this issue. First of all, when you talk about CEOs, you're talking about such a miniscule percentage of the population; the culture is in a tremendous upheaval and all we talk about is a tiny slice at the top. And it's unimaginative because, yes, you can take a snapshot right now and see that there are many more male CEOs, but what I am talking about is a trend dating back forty years. Men have been in power for, like, 40,000 years or, as Caitlin says, 100,000 years. So it's not like there has been a grand revolution and everything will flip overnight. If it had happened that way we would have read about it in the papers, it would have even driven Rob Ford out of the papers; that, if nothing else.

RUDYARD GRIFFITHS: But when you see those lines for women going up into the future and male performance lines going down, do you think there is a revolution for women out there at some point? Maybe in 2050 or 2100? Do you think we need some big, societal change?

HANNA ROSIN: This is where I'm hesitant. I'm totally not hesitant about the cultural change, the change in the structure of families, the change in the way men and women regard each other. I have become very hesitant about the change at the very top because I don't like to construct this argument such that women become men, like the world flips in a totally predictable way, where women want to become CEOs. They don't. I mean, women are different than men, they have a different sense of where power comes from, of how power, aspiration, and ambition work, so they don't just want to be the head of Fortune 500 companies. It's not the way women are built. Power comes in all different ways; maybe the economy will change to accommodate that. I'm not really sure how it will turn out, but it's not as simple as men stay home and take care of the children and women become CEOs. There is no way it will play out in that way.

RUDYARD GRIFFITHS: Not a world of Amazons?

HANNA ROSIN: No.

RUDYARD GRIFFITHS: Well, Hanna Rosin, thank you so much for your time today.

HANNA ROSIN: Thank you.

CAMILLE PAGLIA IN CONVERSATION
WITH RUDYARD GRIFFITHS

RUDYARD GRIFFITHS: I'm here with Camille Paglia. She is an academic and iconic writer, known for a number of bestselling books. And also — I love this, Camille — you are also a columnist for the *Hollywood Reporter*.

CAMILLE PAGLIA: I'm not a columnist, but I do write for them. I run the gamut. I became very interested in popular culture at a time when being interested in Hollywood or rock and roll was considered unserious. There is absolutely no doubt that I lost credibility in grad school at Yale because of my passion for movies. I mean European art films were basically unknown at that point.

RUDYARD GRIFFITHS: I want you to expand on one of your many quotable quotes: "Feminism was wrong to pretend that women could 'have it all.' It's not male society but Mother Nature that lays the heaviest burden on women."

CAMILLE PAGLIA: Yes, it was the theme of my first book, *Sexual Personae*. I came to this conclusion through a long search process. As a dissident personality, I did not identify at all with my gender role as a child and blamed society for everything. Through the course of study and research I began to understand that it is actually Mother Nature who is still women's greatest obstacle because women still bear the burden of pregnancy and of nursing. So I think that women who choose to have children have categorically different lives than men, who can take on fatherhood almost as sort of a social duty, as a social responsibility. But a woman who is pregnant is involved with a fetus in a way that is absolutely primal and instinctual: there are biological forces that take her over. If you raise this issue with feminists today, 99 percent of them squawk and scream and say that this is a conservative, reactionary position. No, this is a realistic position. Feminism is in a state of delusion and losing ground the longer it denies this overwhelming fact of nature. I agree with the Marquis de Sade, Oscar Wilde, Baudelaire, and Gautier — my masters — that it is our obligation as human beings to defy nature if necessary, but one cannot deny nature's power, nature's existence. Universities around the world now teach this rot that gender is nothing but a fiction, an arbitrary convention —

RUDYARD GRIFFITHS: A construct.

CAMILLE PAGLIA: Yes, they would use that word: construct. They teach the idea that gender is imposed, and I believe this is absolute madness. How will we differentiate between the genders?

I support everything transgender. I call my feminism "drag queen feminism," so in no way am I coming from the right-wing side. But what I am saying is that it is about time for feminist discourse to re-appropriate biology. Biology must be a required course in every women's studies or gender studies program. The absence of biology has produced propagandists, people who have never even thought about science. They're incompetents and that is why there is so much confusion and why most people don't care about the women's movement — it is so divorced from reality.

RUDYARD GRIFFITHS: Give us a bit of the flavour of your talk tonight. You are an admirer of what a lot of men have built culturally and you think it is key to how we need to understand civilization, not just in the past, not just today, but in the future.

CAMILLE PAGLIA: "If civilization had been left in female hands, we would still be living in grass huts" was one of my most inflammatory statements in *Sexual Personae*. But no one thought through what I was saying. I was saying, in effect, that all of the greatest works of life-defying, risk-taking enterprises have been the products of men. *Sexual Personae* presented the thesis that men have been driven to create because of their more ambiguous sense of identity. Women know who they are from the moment their menstruation begins at puberty. They don't have to prove it. But men always have to prove it: again, and again, and again, with every erection. Heterosexual men in particular. They wander the world, finally finding the woman of their dreams, and it ends up just being a vision of their mother. And the sex act is going back to the womb. There's a terrifying aspect to sex with all kinds of dark, imaginative forces going on beneath the surface that feminism kind of ignores.

So yes, I have learned enormously from men, but one of my other sentences from that book is, "There is no female Mozart because there is no female Jack the Ripper." I'm saying that women cluster at the median point of the intelligence ranks; they do not produce great geniuses, nor do they produce the morons, criminals, and mass murderers. Men are overwhelmingly the people who pick up guns and weapons and massacre children, acting out distorted fantasies that emerge from the male mind. Every act of genius has its corollary in an act of madness. So again, I think feminism has been so concerned to deny sexual differences that it has painted itself into a corner. The feminist movement is, right now, moribund. It is moribund because ordinary people feel that feminists have nothing to say to their passions, their concerns, and their desires. So it's time to bring feminism back to the real world, re-examine biology again, and be fair to men. Enough of this negativity toward men.

RUDYARD GRIFFITHS: Interesting. Let me end by asking you a question I've asked some of the other presenters here tonight. Is there a man — an icon fictional or real, a director or writer — who you think really gets women right?

CAMILLE PAGLIA: My favourite director is Alfred Hitchcock. I wrote a book on *The Birds* for the British Film Institute. Feminists have notoriously pilloried Hitchcock as a misogynist, but I think he had it right. From my perspective, as a marginalized and always-complaining lesbian, I really think that Hitchcock had an eye for beautiful and sexy women and understood their relationship to their bodies, to presentation, and to costume — the kind of glamorous, sexual woman that feminism has never taken seriously and has always attacked as being merely a pawn of male fantasy. And that is not what I see at all — I am extremely interested in very beautiful, glamorous women.

RUDYARD GRIFFITHS: Why? Do you see power there?

CAMILLE PAGLIA: I am a great fan of the Bravo series *The Real Housewives*; the executive producer is a gay man, Andy Cohen, who grew up watching Susan Lucci on *All My Children*. He's a big fan of soap opera. Soap opera was part of the lineage coming from Hollywood: the women's pictures and the suffering, glamorous stars like Lana Turner. And I have said that *The Real Housewives*, a reality show, is an anthropological study of the actual way beautiful, sexy women interrelate. It's absolutely a universal. And feminism cannot handle it. Gloria Steinem said she wanted to picket *The Real Housewives* shows, which demonstrates the gap between her and me. I watch these shows; I can watch an episode four or five times.

Wherever I go in the world, I see beautiful women acting toward each other in exactly the same way. It's women who appreciate how a woman dresses. Women dress for other women. What do men know? Men know nothing! Men just say, "Oh, you look nice." Women say, "You look beautiful." Women immediately assess each other because there is tremendous sexual competition between high-profile women that feminism has been afraid to acknowledge because the movement would have to admit that women are bitches, and women are catty. Well that's just too bad. Yes, I do worship the beautiful, glamorous woman. Time does conquer all and beauty fades, which is why we value it. The ancient Greeks loved beautiful boys with beautiful, perfect bodies. So to me, it is a failure of feminism that it cannot acknowledge that beauty is a value in itself. Even if a woman managed to achieve beauty for a particular moment, she has contributed something to the culture. And thank heavens for photography and for movies that preserve the beauty of certain women at their absolute peak forever, whether it's Catherine Deneuve or Elizabeth Taylor, or Jean Harlow and Rita Hayworth, the great stars of the 1930s and 1940s. So my entire frame of reference is closer to that of the mass audience that goes to movies than it is to that of feminist theorists.

RUDYARD GRIFFITHS: Well, Camille, you've given us a terrific taste of what we're going to hear tonight —

CAMILLE PAGLIA: No, no, I have to be polite tonight. This is a Canadian audience and I must rein myself in.

RUDYARD GRIFFITHS: Just don't do what Canadians do, which is to start violently agreeing with each other. I'm counting on you.

CAMILLE PAGLIA: Alright, Rudyard.

RUDYARD GRIFFITHS: Thanks for your time.

Post-Debate Commentary

POST-DEBATE COMMENTARY
BY CHRISTINA HOFF SOMMERS

"Be it resolved that men are obsolete." That was the question last week at a high-spirited edition of Toronto's celebrated Munk Debates. Hanna Rosin and Maureen Dowd said, "OMG yes!" Camille Paglia and Caitlin Moran: "No way!"

To men offended by the proposition: lighten up. Don't join those censorious feminists who have made the battle of the sexes a humour-free zone.

Rosin opened by asking, "How do we know men are finished?" Her answer was a quote from embattled Toronto mayor Rob Ford. "Yeah, there have been times I have been in a drunken stupor." Exhibit B for her argument that men have become as fussy and insecure as women was a tweeted photograph of Anthony Weiner's meticulously waxed chest. Along the way, she made serious points about how men are falling behind in education and the workplace. Women are adapting in the new world of gender equality; men are not. "Men are the new ball and chain," Rosin said.

Paglia was having none of it. She reminded Rosin and the female supremacists that their busy alpha-female lives are made possible by an invisible army of men — "men who do the dirty, dangerous work of building roads, pouring concrete, laying bricks, tarring roofs, hanging electric wires, excavating natural gas and sewage lines, cutting and clearing trees, and bulldozing the landscape for housing developments." Paglia described the modern economy, with its vast system of production and distribution, as a sublime "male epic." Women have joined it — but men built it. "Surely," said the fiery Paglia, "modern women are strong enough now to give credit where credit is due!" And she reminded women that without strong men as models to either embrace or reject, women will never attain a distinctive sense of themselves *as* women.

Maureen Dowd made good fun of her misfortune in following Camille Paglia, beginning, "I've never debated before, and I am so screwed." She did not fully engage the topic, but her beguiling style was a caution against letting "men and women are identical" ideologues drive the discussion. With her Veronica Lake hair and slinky black dress, Dowd was an alluring 1940s-style vamp with up-to-date female taunts: "Men are so last century . . . they seemed to have stopped evolving." When guys finally exit the stage, she wondered if they would be taking "video games, *Game of Thrones* on continuous loop, and cold pizza in the morning with them." "Women," said Dowd, have "clicked their ruby stilettos three times" and now realize they are in charge. "The world is not flat, Tom Friedman. The world is curvy." Actually, the world is both — as Dowd clearly knows and enjoys. And she does not want to destroy men; she wants to have fun with them while joining them in the pursuit of power and happiness. Her playful, *femme fatale* feminism was more appealing than anything in Women's Studies 101.

Caitlin Moran, British writer and humorist, began by warning that her feminism was strident, Marxist, and "fuelled by cocktails." But she turned out to be a down-to-earth humanist, reminding everyone that calling men obsolete was no better than the bad old sexist days when women were said to be irrelevant. We are in this together, said Moran: if one sex fails, the other staggers. All of the speakers acknowledged that working-class men's fortunes have fallen and that boys are having serious difficulties in schools. But, Moran insisted, that does not mean we should celebrate their travails, but rather that we should do everything possible to improve their prospects. She shocked and delighted the audience with her concluding remark: "Are men obsolete? My answer is *no*! I won't let you be, you fuckers!"

Imagine four brilliant, accomplished, funny women discussing the politics of gender outside the dreary, angry, "rape-culture"-obsessed framework of contemporary feminism. That happened this past Friday night at the Munk Debate, and both sexes came out ahead in the encounter.

Christina Hoff Sommers is a resident scholar at the American Enterprise Institute and the author of The War Against Boys.

POST-DEBATE COMMENTARY
BY STEPHANIE COONTZ

The debaters were witty and articulate, but their claims were often contradictory. While the audience may have had fun, they received little accurate information.

Defenders of the proposition that men are obsolete told us that women are becoming the dominant sex. Sometimes Hanna Rosin and Maureen Dowd portrayed men as slackers and sulkers, holding up Toronto's hapless mayor as an exemplar of the modern male. At other times (joined by Camille Paglia), they depicted men as the unfortunate victims of feminized schools, feminist harridans, and man-eating *femmes fatales.*

On the "con" side, Caitlin Moran countered that patriarchy is still alive and well, claiming that men hold 99 percent of the world's wealth. Camille Paglia argued that we should shore up masculinity because we still need men to defend our turf, do the dirty work that keeps industrial societies going, and let us focus on being women.

What are the facts? Women have indeed made dramatic progress in overturning discriminatory barriers, but they have not become the richer sex, even in the most advanced industrial nations. Women's wages climbed faster than men's for the past three decades, but they started from a much lower base and still have not caught up. The median hourly wage for women in the U.S. rose from less than 63 percent that of men in 1979 to almost 83 percent by 2012. But on average a woman needs to work fifty-two years to earn the same income a man can make in forty years.

Today women earn nearly 60 percent of university degrees, and a female college graduate's salary is typically higher than a male high-school graduate's, unlike decades past. Yet at every educational level, full-time female workers still earn less than men with the *same* credentials.

That said, we are certainly not in the grip of a millennium-old patriarchy. Moran rightly pointed out the continuing worldwide subjugation of women, but her claim that men own 99 percent of the world's wealth is wrong. Even ignoring the joint property rights that married women have won, and excluding all the female entrepreneurs and heiresses around the world, sociologist Philip Cohen calculates that unmarried women in the U.S. alone earn more than one percent of the world's total wealth.

Men in advanced industrial societies have lost or voluntarily relinquished many traditional patriarchal prerogatives. In the U.S., domestic violence rates have declined by 53 percent since the early 1990s, and sexual assaults have dropped by 70 percent. Married men have tripled the time they spend on childcare and housework since the 1960s.

A less positive aspect of changing gender relations is that in many countries women's relative improvement in employment stems less from their absolute progress than from men's losses. In the United States, more than a quarter of women's gains relative to men result from men's declining wages.

Inequality between high- and low-wage earners has been growing for women and men alike, with destabilizing effects on individuals and families. Yet too many people think it's obsolete to insist that people who do the less-skilled but essential work in our economies — janitors, industrial workers, retail clerks, food workers — deserve a living wage, along with social protections that allow them to meet family obligations.

I agree with Camille Paglia that we ought to revalue the trades where men once earned a secure living. But we should equally value the work performed by nursery school teachers, health-care aides, secretaries, and daycare workers. Reviving traditional notions of masculinity is not the way to revitalize working-class communities. In fact, such notions increasingly hold men back. Most of the problems boys have in school stem from the retrograde masculine mystique that "real boys" don't study. One reason for men's lower enrolment and higher dropout rates in college is the assumption that men do not need as much education as women in order to make a good living.

Old forms of gender advantage often backfire today. Men who drop out of college earn entry-level salaries comparable to those of male college graduates. Women dropouts, by contrast, are immediately penalized, with starting salaries on average $6,500 per year less than women college grads. But this initial gender "privilege" for men imposes heavy long-term costs. By midlife, most male college dropouts earn less than college graduates of either gender.

Men are not obsolete. What are obsolete are the twin notions that men and women have different needs, capacities, and values, and that the rise of women is a threat to men. As Caitlin Moran pointed out, we're in this together. The closer women get to equality, the better off are their partners, sons, and brothers.

Stephanie Coontz teaches at Evergreen State College in Olympia, Washington, and is Director of Research and Public Education at the Council on Contemporary Families.

ACKNOWLEDGEMENTS

The Munk Debates are the product of the public-spiritedness of a remarkable group of civic-minded organizations and individuals. First and foremost, these debates would not be possible without the vision and leadership of the Aurea Foundation. Founded in 2006 by Peter and Melanie Munk, the Aurea Foundation supports Canadian individuals and institutions involved in the study and development of public policy. The debates are the foundation's signature initiative, a model for the kind of substantive public policy conversation Canadians can foster globally. Since the creation of the debates in 2008, the foundation has underwritten the entire cost of each semi-annual event. The debates have also benefited from the input and advice of members of the board of the foundation, including Mark Cameron, Andrew Coyne, Devon Cross, Allan Gotlieb, George Jonas, Margaret MacMillan, Anthony Munk, and Janice Stein.

For her contribution to the preliminary edit of the book, the debate organizers would like to thank Jane McWhinney.

Since their inception the Munk Debates have sought to take the discussions that happen at each event to national and international audiences. Here the debates have benefited immeasurably from a partnership with Canada's national newspaper, the *Globe and Mail*, and the counsel of its editor-in-chief, John Stackhouse.

With the publication of this superb book, House of Anansi Press is helping the debates reach new audiences in Canada and internationally. The debates' organizers would like to thank Anansi chair, Scott Griffin, and president and publisher, Sarah MacLachlan, for their enthusiasm for this book project and insights into how to translate the spoken debate into a powerful written intellectual exchange.

ABOUT THE DEBATERS

HANNA ROSIN is the author of *The End of Men*, the definitive book on the decline of men and maleness in modern society. She is a national correspondent at *The Atlantic*, where she writes broadly about American culture; a writer and editor for *Slate*; and a founder and editor of *DoubleX, Slate*'s site for women. She has written for *The New Yorker*, the *New York Times, GQ, The New Republic*, and the *Washington Post*. A National Magazine Award winner, her stories have been included in the anthologies *Best American Magazine Writing* and *Best American Crime Reporting*. Hanna Rosin lives in Washington, D.C., with her husband and their three children.

MAUREEN DOWD is the winner of a Pulitzer Prize for distinguished commentary and the author of *Are Men Necessary?* She has been a *New York Times* op-ed columnist since 1995, after serving as a correspondent in the paper's Washington bureau since 1996. She has covered four presidential campaigns for the *New York Times* and has served as White House correspondent. She is regularly ranked among the top hundred public intellectuals in America. Maureen Dowd lives in New York City.

CAITLIN MORAN is a British broadcaster, TV critic, and writer for *The Times* of London. Named Columnist of the Year in 2010 and both Critic and Interviewer of the Year in 2011 by the British Awards, she is the author of the global bestseller *How To Be a Woman*. The *New York Times* called the book a "glorious, timely stand against sexism so ingrained we barely notice it . . . a book that needed to be written." It has been published in twenty-three languages. Caitlin Moran lives on Twitter with her husband and two children.

CAMILLE PAGLIA is recognized as one of the world's top hundred public intellectuals by *Foreign Policy* and *Prospect*. She is currently a professor of humanities and media studies at the University of the Arts in Philadelphia. Her book *Sexual Personae: Art and Decadence from Nefertiti to Emily Dickinson* is considered an iconic work of literary criticism. Her other books include *Sex, Art, and American Culture*, *Break, Blow, Burn*, and *Glittering Images: A Journey Through Art from Egypt to Star Wars*. She was a co-founding contributor and columnist for *Salon* and has written numerous articles on art, literature, popular culture, feminism, politics, and religion for publications around the world. Camille Paglia lives in Philadelphia, Pennsylvania.

ABOUT THE EDITOR

RUDYARD GRIFFITHS is the organizer and moderator of the Munk Debates. In 2006 he was named one of Canada's "Top 40 under 40" by the *Globe and Mail.* He is the editor of thirteen books on history, politics, and international affairs and author of *Who We Are: A Citizen's Manifesto,* which was a *Globe and Mail* Best Book of 2009 and a finalist for the Shaughnessy Cohen Prize for Political Writing. He lives in Toronto with his wife and two children.

ABOUT THE MUNK DEBATES

The Munk Debates are Canada's premier public policy event. Held semi-annually, the debates provide leading thinkers with a global forum to discuss the major public policy issues facing the world and Canada. Each event takes place in Toronto in front of a live audience, and the proceedings are covered by domestic and international media. Participants in recent Munk Debates include Robert Bell, Tony Blair, John Bolton, Ian Bremmer, Daniel Cohn-Bendit, Paul Collier, Howard Dean, Hernando de Soto, Gareth Evans, Mia Farrow, Niall Ferguson, William Frist, Newt Gingrich, David Gratzer, Rick Hillier, Christopher Hitchens, Richard Holbrooke, Josef Joffe, Henry Kissinger, Charles Krauthammer, Paul Krugman, Arthur Laffer, Lord Nigel Lawson, Stephen Lewis, David Li, Bjørn Lomborg, Lord Peter Mandelson, Elizabeth May, George Monbiot,

Dambisa Moyo, Vali Nasr, George Papandreou, Samantha Power, David Rosenberg, Lawrence Summers, Amos Yadlin, and Fareed Zakaria.

The Munk Debates are a project of the Aurea Foundation, a charitable organization established in 2006 by philanthropists Peter and Melanie Munk to promote public policy research and discussion. For more information, visit www.munkdebates.com.

ABOUT THE INTERVIEWS

Rudyard Griffith's interviews with Caitlin Moran, Maureen Dowd, Hanna Rosin, and Camille Paglia were recorded on November 15, 2013. The Aurea Foundation is gratefully acknowledged for permission to reprint excerpts from the following:

(p. 53) "Caitlin Moran in Conversation," by Rudyard Griffiths. Copyright 2013 Aurea Foundation. Transcribed by Rondi Adamson.

(p. 63) "Maureen Dowd in Conversation," by Rudyard Griffiths. Copyright 2013 Aurea Foundation. Transcribed by Rondi Adamson.

(p. 67) "Hanna Rosin in Conversation," by Rudyard Griffiths. Copyright 2013 Aurea Foundation. Transcribed by Rondi Adamson.

(p. 75) "Camille Paglia in Conversation," by Rudyard Griffiths. Copyright 2013 Aurea Foundation. Transcribed by Rondi Adamson.

ABOUT THE POST-DEBATE COMMENTARY

The post-debate commentaries by Christina Hoff Sommers and Stephanie Coontz were written on November 16, 2013. The Aurea Foundation wishes to thank Ali Wyne for his assistance in commissioning these essays.

Should We Tax the Rich More?

Krugman and Papandreou vs. Gingrich and Laffer

Is imposing higher taxes on the wealthy the best way for countries to reinvest in their social safety nets, education, and infrastructure while protecting the middle class? Or does raising taxes on society's wealth creators lead to capital flight, falling government revenues, and less money for the poor? Nobel Prize–winning economist Paul Krugman and former prime minister of Greece George Papandreou square off against former Speaker of the U.S. House of Representatives Newt Gingrich and famed economist Arthur Laffer to debate this key issue.

"The effort to finance big government through higher taxes is a direct assault on civil society."

— Newt Gingrich

Can the World Tolerate an Iran with Nuclear Weapons?

Krauthammer and Yadlin vs. Zakaria and Nasr

Is the case for a pre-emptive strike on Iran ironclad? Or can a nuclear Iran be a stabilizing force in the Middle East? Former Israel Defense Forces head of military intelligence Amos Yadlin, Pulitzer Prize–winning political commentator Charles Krauthammer, CNN host Fareed Zakaria, and Iranian-born academic Vali Nasr debate the consequences of a nuclear-armed Iran.

"Deterring Iran is fundamentally different from deterring the Soviet Union. You could rely on the latter but not the former."
— Charles Krauthammer

Has the European Experiment Failed?
Joffe and Ferguson vs. Mandelson and Cohn-Bendit

Is one of human history's most ambitious endeavours nearing collapse? Former EU Commissioner for Trade Peter Mandelson and EU Parliament co-president of the Greens/European Free Alliance Group Daniel Cohn-Bendit debate German publisher-editor and author Josef Joffe and renowned economic historian Niall Ferguson on the future of the European Union.

"For more than ten years, it has been the case that Europe has conducted an experiment in the impossible."

— Niall Ferguson

North America's Lost Decade?

Krugman and Rosenberg vs. Summers and Bremmer

The future of the North American economy is more uncertain than ever. In this edition of the Munk Debates, Nobel Prize–winning economist Paul Krugman and chief economist and strategist at Gluskin Sheff + Associates David Rosenberg square off against former U.S. Treasury secretary Lawrence Summers and bestselling author Ian Bremmer to tackle the resolution: Be it resolved North America faces a Japan-style era of high unemployment and slow growth.

"It's now impossible to deny the obvious, which is that we are not now, and have never been, on the road to recovery."
— Paul Krugman

www.houseofanansi.com/munkdebates

Does the 21st Century Belong to China?

Kissinger and Zakaria vs. Ferguson and Li

Is China's rise unstoppable? Former U.S. Secretary of State Henry Kissinger and CNN's Fareed Zakaria pair off against leading historian Niall Ferguson and world-renowned Chinese economist David Daokui Li to debate China's emergence as a global force, the key geopolitical issue of our time.

This edition of The Munk Debate on China is the first formal public debate Dr. Kissinger has participated in on China's future.

"I have enormous difficulty imagining a world dominated by China . . . I believe the concept that any one country will dominate the world is, in itself, a misunderstanding of the world in which we live now."

— Henry Kissinger

Hitchens vs. Blair

Christopher Hitchens vs. Tony Blair

Intellectual juggernaut and staunch atheist Christopher Hitchens goes head-to-head with former British prime minister Tony Blair, one of the Western world's most openly devout political leaders, on the age-old question: Is religion a force for good in the world? Few world leaders have had a greater hand in shaping current events than Blair; few writers have been more outspoken and polarizing than Hitchens.

Sharp, provocative, and thoroughly engrossing, *Hitchens vs. Blair* is a rigorous and electrifying intellectual sparring match on the contentious questions that continue to dog the topic of religion in our globalized world.

"If religious instruction were not allowed until the child had attained the age of reason, we would be living in a very different world."

— Christopher Hitchens

The Munk Debates: Volume One

Edited by Rudyard Griffiths; Introduction by Peter Munk

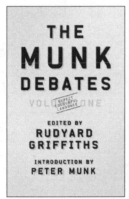

Launched in 2008 by philanthropists Peter and Melanie Munk, the Munk Debates is Canada's premier international debate series, a highly anticipated cultural event that brings together the world's brightest minds.

This volume includes the first five debates in the series, and features twenty leading thinkers and doers arguing for or against provocative resolutions that address pressing public policy concerns, such as the future of global security, the implications of humanitarian intervention, the effectiveness of foreign aid, the threat of climate change, and the state of health care in Canada and the United States.

"By trying to highlight the most important issues at crucial moments in the global conversation, these debates not only profile the ideas and solutions of some of our brightest thinkers and doers, but crystallize public passion and knowledge, helping to tackle some global challenges confronting humankind."

— Peter Munk

www.houseofanansi.com/munkdebates